AF574112

INDIANS in the ROCKIES

Box 490, Banff, Alberta, Canada, TOL OCO

ISBN 0-919381-15-4
Design: Scott Thornley, Bruce Aitken
Art Production: Alyson Hannas, Dave Thompson
Typesetting: Crocker Bryant Inc.
Colour Separations: Dai Nippon
Printed and Bound in Japan

Canadian Cataloguing in Publication Data

Whyte, Jon, 1941–
Indians in the Rockies

"Sponsored by the Banff Indian Days Association."
Includes index.
Bibliography: p. 127
ISBN 0-919381-15-4

1. Indians of North America – Rocky Mountain Region – History. 2. Assiniboine Indians – History. 3. Rocky Mountain Region – History. 4. Indians of North America – Pictorial works. I. Banff Indian Days Association. II. Title.
E78.A34W49 1984   970.004'97   C84-091399-0

INDIANS in the ROCKIES

Jon Whyte

sponsored by
The Banff Indian Days Association

Foreword by the Honourable Ralph G. Steinhauer

A

Altitude Publishing Ltd.
1985

For John Mountain Stoney
son of Mark Poucette
and all the people of the Rockies
who contributed
to Banff Indian Days

The White boys, Dave White junior and Peter, with Mark Poucette's son, circa 1914. The Stoney boy died shortly after the photo was taken. In 1915 Mark Poucette adopted little Dave – whom Banffites called Jack or Jackie – as his son John Mountain Stoney.
Photographer unknown, photo courtesy the Whyte Museum of the Canadian Rockies.

Contents

Sampson and Leah Beaver with their daughter Frances Louise, Kootenay Plains, North Saskatchewan River, 1907. Mary T.S. Schäffer, a Philadelphia-born author, photographer, and botanist, undertook major outfitted pack trips in the Rockies north of the CPR main line. Using a map Sampson Beaver provided for her in 1907, she explored Maligne Lake in 1908 in what is now Jasper National Park, writing about her experiences in *Old Indian Trails*. Photo by Mary T.S. Schäffer, courtesy the Whyte Museum of the Canadian Rockies.

John Simeon, Eli Rider, Eli Rider's mother, John Salter, and Ben Kaquitts; Banff Indian Days, circa 1910. The individual and unique costumes the Stoney wore during the Banff festival were authentic. Photographers never dressed their subjects in clothing they believed more colourful. Photo, circa 1910, by Byron Harmon, courtesy the Whyte Museum of the Canadian Rockies.

Foreword

This is a story that needed telling, the story of the beginnings of Banff and the story of the Indian people of the area, their intricate involvement with mountains, and with the white people who brought changes to that area.

The Indians of the eastern slopes of the Canadian Rockies and the nearby plains hunted in the mountain valleys, gathered medicinal herbs which grew there, and gathered together at appointed times for religious ceremonies. For them the mountains were a place of mystery where spirits dwelt, the hot springs were healing waters. The Indians went to the mountains seeking both spiritual and physical renewal.

Momentous changes in the country forced the Indians to change their way of life. The coming of the white traders and the decimation of the buffalo herds weakened the foundations of their lifestyle. The influx of white settlement and the signing of the treaties together with the building of the railroad brought about a total upheaval in all they had experienced up to that time. With the establishment of the National Parks, they found themselves almost totally cut off from access to the mountains.

The Indian people became mere spectators of the development around them, and they slipped into a condition of apathy for the most part. The founding of Banff Indian Days brought contact with the world outside the reserves, as did taking part in Calgary Stampede activities. Indian people dearly love a celebration, and in this way are very like their white brothers. A gathering such as Banff Indian Days meant an extended visit with relatives and friends from near and far. It meant also an opportunity to commune with the spirits, for the mountains were—and still are—a place for meditation and prayer, a place to contemplate a possible course of action or change of direction in life.

The lives of the Indians were suited to the country. Their culture also evolved to fit the environment. They can no longer live the old way, and are trying desperately to learn the new ways of a lifestyle which is foreign to them, while still struggling to retain some of their own culture.

I hope this book wakens those who read it to an understanding of the unforeseen hardships inflicted on the Indian people because of the forced transition from a beloved way of life to one so totally different.

Ralph G. Steinhauer
Brosseau, Alberta

Mr. Steinhauer served as Lieutenant-Governor of Alberta from 1974 to 1979. Born at Morley, Alberta, in 1905, he was the first Indian to serve as the Queen's representative in Canada. He was also a councillor on the Saddle Lake Reserve, Alberta, for 34 years.

"At the gate of the mountains," by Captain Henry James Warre, 1845, watercolour. Parties crossing the mountains relied on the technology of the region's ancient residents. Warre painted his exaggerated view of the peaks near Morley as he entered the Rockies.
Courtesy the Public Archives of Canada.

Invocation

I will sing to the Lizard, the Great One of the Mountains.
I will sing to the many, his sons and his daughters.
Let them roll over mountain slopes,
slither down hillsides,
gliding down, splintering trees,
turning snow into streams,
powdering rocks into sand grains and dust.

Look, now, he comes, the Great One of the Mountains,
his children following him.

Now they sit ringing him,
loosening the bands on their brows.
A wind from the canyon blows the bands upwards.
Look, and look with me!
The bands become rainbows,
wonderful rainbows
from the Earth arcing up to the sky!
Their breathing, their sighing, the breath of the Lizards
from mountain tops singing:

"The breath of our bodies becomes rainbows;
healing and cleansing.
Behold us, arcs of pure colour.
Look, look at us, look at the rainbows,
the mountain's breath, Lizard's breath, and be whole."

adapted from a Salish Medicine Man's invocation,
recorded by Marius Barbeau

Mark Poucette, Stoney. His wide bow is typically Stoney. The strung brass beads forming his breastplate became common in the late nineteenth century.
Portrait, circa 1910, by Byron Harmon, courtesy the Whyte Museum of the Canadian Rockies.

Introduction

"On your Mark Poucette, go!"

That's how, when I was a little kid in the 1940s in Banff, we started our foot races.

Our family revered Mark Poucette, a Stoney. An old man when I met him, Mark was one of the few Stoney men who still wore their hair in braids. About 1975 I met his grandson Mark, then about ten, proudly wearing his hair in braids. A new veneration for the ways of their elders was expressing itself in a new generation.

Old Mark Poucette had been a friend of my grandfather. Dave White arrived in the Rockies in April, 1886, and that year became the CPR section man at Sawback, eleven kilometres west of Banff. A century ago, Stoney families were still making their slow trek up the Bow Valley from the Morley Reserve in the Rocky Mountain foothills, crossing the Great Divide to hunt in the headwaters of the Kootenay River on the western slope of the Rockies. A traditional ford on the Bow River lay close by my grandfather's section house, so the Stoney pattern soon included stopping in for tea and conversation on their way over and back. Eight years later, when Papa—as we refer to him in the family—started the Park Store, a general store in Banff, the Stoney Indians continued to drop in. (Family legend says Dave adopted "White" because it was less bother to change his name than to get a signpainter to come up from Calgary again to correct the error he had made in the sign while Dave was making a delivery to the nearby mining town of Bankhead.)

My father Dave, my uncles Clifford and Peter, and my aunt Lila grew up in a home where the Poucettes, the Wildman family, the McLeans, the Bearspaws, and their kin frequently visited. One of my uncle Pete's favourite stories concerned a visit to the White home by a Norwegian ski-jumper friend. Mark Poucette was there, and the opportunity to meet and talk with an Indian fascinated the Norwegian. A perplexed Mark finally said to the Scandinavian, "I don't understand you. You look like a white man, but you talk like a Chinaman."

For a decade or more Papa annually disbursed the Treaty Money at Morley and my father and uncles got to know the reserve and their Stoney friends in an at-home context on those trips to Morley. Papa often made up food bundles for his friends on the reserve to help them through the tough parts of the winter. He did as much for the villagers in Banff's boom and bust economy.

Mark Poucette and his wife suffered a tragedy when disease carried away their sons. The heartbroken chief came to Dave White with an unusual request. He wished to adopt my father into his family. In 1914, when my father was seven, in a simple, private, and moving ceremony, he became John Mountain Stoney, son of Mark Poucette.

In the 1930s my uncle Peter and his wife, Catharine, whom he met at art school in Boston, undertook a series of Stoney portraits, several of which I've used in this book. Catharine, a fine amateur historian, wrote down many of the stories she and Pete learned from the Stoneys while they were painting them. My book owes a great deal to Catharine's accurate reporting. Admirers of Stoney art, Pete and Catharine assembled a significant collection of costumes, beadwork, and Stoney artifacts.

Imbued with respect for the Stoney People since my earliest memories, I undertook this book with a slight hesitation. Wishing to honour Stoney traditions, I wanted to write an informal history placing the Stoney in a larger context, the human history of the Canadian Rockies and the surrounding region. Neither ethnographer nor historian, I'm a poet familiar with the region, and a sometime journalist who has a love for story and some respect for facts. I was born in Banff, and I love the mountains and their people, reasons I believe sufficient for my undertaking this book.

For *Indians in the Rockies* I had to put together divers accounts of the story. Two things quickly became apparent to me: first, how well the Paleo-Indians and Indians knew the geography of the region; second, how few fur traders who mapped the Rockies' rivers and passes made claims they discovered anything. Fur traders like Alexander Mackenzie, Peter Fidler, David Thompson, and others sought quick and easy routes from the east side of the mountains to the west; Indians who knew the mountains well showed them the way. The fable of the mountain barrier awaited the nineteenth century, when the demand grew for moving huge amounts of material through the mountains and for finding a route for the Canadian Pacific Railway.

This volume serves as prologue to the standard history of the region. I've tried, not deceitfully but with some consideration for craft, to place Indians in the Rockies before the fur traders, missionaries, treaty makers, railroad builders, and tourists intruded upon them. The intruders usually wrote the sources, and their bias is implicit in what they wrote. Trying to eliminate most of the bias and sift the facts from the opinion, I can never imagine with more than a modicum of accuracy how the Kootenay, Cree, Shuswap, or Stoney first saw the strangers from the east. My aunt's notes and the ethnographic story collecting of Marius Barbeau at Morley in the 1920s have been the checks against which I have tried to prove my version of the history.

I advise the reader seeking an ethnological treatment of the subject to look elsewhere. Without the knowledge of able experts—people like the Getty brothers, who have worked with the Stoney, and Claude E. Schaeffer, who was the Curator of the Plains Indian Museum in Browning, Montana, a major ethnographer of the Kootenay—in ethnology, ethnography, archaeology, and geography, I could never have written this book. I did not intend to usurp their knowledge without sincerely expressing how important I think their work has been.

Since this is an attempt to assemble a disparate and scattered geography of many different nations and language groups, I'm sure I shall offend or displease some groups. Rest assured, I did not intend to offend. Speculation honestly expressed can lead to illumination, and if I occasionally suggest new routes for both Indian and non-Indian historians to explore, I shall be pleased. I have retold some of the more hair-raising stories the Stoney told Dr Barbeau, not to shock, but because they provide a vivid rendering of the Stoney self-image. Regretfully, no Marius Barbeau recorded in like liveliness what other groups, the Rocky Mountain Cree for example, or the Shuswap in the Yellowhead Pass or the Sarcee near Calgary, said about their legendary past. It may not yet be too late for someone to find remnants of those legends, but time ravages rather than distills legend.

I've tried to keep my spelling consistent. Anyone who has read the accounts of fur traders like David Thompson or missionaries like John McDougall knows the hundred-plus ways to spell Assiniboine, the two or three ways of spelling Stoney and Kootenay. If I've ignored the spelling currently in vogue, I thought it better to be consistent than fashionable. I have chosen, however, to use the term Déné for the tribes once referred to as Athapaskan-speaking: the Sekani, Slavey, Beaver, Sarcee, and other nations of the north, and the linguistically-related tribes of the American southwest, the Navajo and Apache. The name they prefer themselves, Déné replaces the word Athapaskan, which was taken from the Cree language meaning "people of the reeds."

If the book suffers an imbalance, it is its emphasis upon the Stoney People in the past century. They are closest to me, I know them best, and more documents about them were available to me. I mean no disservice to the peoples of other tribes.

Some readers may wish I devoted more words to the politics of famine, the inequities of the reserve system, the Indians' plight in coping with a rapidly changing and still alien society. Others have written those books well; others will write more of them. Not ignorant of the problems, I felt my thoughts would add more to confusion than to discussion.

Wesley Band women, Stoney Indians, near Mount Wilson on the North Saskatchewan River, circa 1920.
Photo by Byron Harmon, courtesy the Whyte Museum of the Canadian Rockies.

Stoney summer encampment, Morley Reserve, circa 1940. Photo by Mrs Nicholas Morant, courtesy the photographer.

1

The First Hundred Centuries

Chill winds blew from the glacier in the main valley. Barren mountain peaks protruded above the ice rivers in the hanging valleys. Scattered grasses and small plants tufted from rock rubble and boulders at the glacier's toe. For two or three kilometres downvalley from the ice few things grew. Murky meltwater from the glacier poured into a lake that extended from the mountain ranges' bases, filling almost the entire width of the valley, dammed by gravel and mud the glacier had piled up. The glacier had withdrawn but recently from that stretch of the valley. Few plants colonized the gravel: rings of dryases, scattered saxifrages, hardier grasses. The glacier, receding thirty to sixty metres per year, was rapidly exposing new ground for plants to colonize.

It was a landscape of titanic dimensions. Upvalley the ice was a kilometre or more deep. Smaller glaciers, contributing to the main valley glacier, tumbled from the cirques they'd carved in the mountains' once sheer slopes. Where two or three glaciers joined to form one valley glacier, long streaked moraines of grit, gravel, and boulders snaked on the surface. Gouged and bulldozed piles of rock, gravel, rough soil, and grime heaped up on the land everywhere. On the valley floor, near where the grumbling river murkily poured from the glacier's snout, a small herd of bison browsed the meagre grasses.

The bison were unaware of a family of hunter-gatherers advancing up the valley in quest of meat. Their tools and weapons they'd rough-hewn from flaky rocks—cherts and flints they'd knapped into points and attached by sinew to hafts of hardwood poles they'd brought from the lower, warmer land on the hills east of the mountains, beside the river's spillway to the plains. Robed in bison hides, as keenly aware of strange sounds and unusual odours as were their prey, the men and women moved stealthily, concealing themselves behind willows or boulders as they advanced, keeping the wind blowing from the animals to them. Should they spook the animals before their hunt had succeeded, they'd waste their day. Hunger burned in their stomachs after the long week of pursuit.

They and their kin had lived in a fierce icy climate for centuries. They had grown up in barren land. Hunger dominated their lives. Feasts were rare. A feast today would relieve their stomachs' torment.

Rough footing on the tangled rock demanded caution. Only at close range did their spears and mauls function. Obtaining food always posed dangers, for they had to close on their prey silently, then kill it cleanly and swiftly, avoiding the sharp horns and the massiveness of the frightened, anguished bison.

They remembered the death of their grandfather who had been the finest stalker of their family, who had yet led a last hunting party after a bull had gored him three summers past. His dying lasted five days after the bull trampled him when, weakened, he could not flee his enraged prey. His sons, good hunters that they were, had not injured the animal swiftly enough.

At the main camp, downvalley a half-day's walk on the lakeshore, the older women gathered roots and berries from bushes growing in the rocky soil. The children, not yet old enough to join the hunting group, played at games which honed their senses. Hide-and-seek was a favourite: practising stealth in sneaking up on each other, standing still behind trees. But other capers involved wrestling dogs to the ground and avoiding the snapping fangs, stretching their muscles boisterously. Always the edge of hunger haunted them. The valley was new to them. Not only to them but to their parents. Occasionally an old one would tell them of the trek south, the journey in the gulf between the glaciers, how they'd crossed the rivers by making ropes of animal hides, how they'd seen no other people for two summers and two winters, how hunger forced them to seek another place where food would provide for everyone, and the possibility—the dream—of a place where hunger would be stayed. The one who peered into his dreams had spoken of it.

Where hunter met prey, the lean one moved forward. A few paces from him now, an old bull drew tufts of seedhead grass from the loose soil. His meat would be tough, but it would feed many. Suddenly the lean one sprang from a higher rock near the bull who was feeding on grasses that grew well in its protection. The man's body bore its weight on the point of the spear, driving it past the blades of the bison's shoulders to soft flesh where it pierced his heart. The bison's mighty bulk heaved as his eyes sought the source of the pain, the dart from heaven so tormenting him, but he could see nothing. While his head was averted, the other hunters leapt in, two of them seizing his hindquarters, and hacking with shorter-handled blades to hamstring him, while others lassoed his legs in sinew ropes. Blood bubbled from the enraged animal's mouth. At his bellow the other animals saw what was happening. Surprisingly fleet of foot, they ran like the wind in the grasses of the valley. In moments no trace of them sullied the air.

The old bull lay dying, the hunters slicing his belly open as his blood ran in the gravel.

The story takes place eight kilometres west of the town of Banff, but it occurred a hundred and fifteen centuries ago. For more than 10,000 years people have travelled the Bow Valley in the Canadian Rockies. For five months in 1983 and again in the summer of 1984 a team of archaeologists explored the region where new highway lanes would run, when the twinning of the Trans-Canada Highway near Banff threatened previously undisturbed ground. In their careful digging the team of fifteen found evidence of the ancient camps. Broken stones and ash, fragments of burned bone, a littering of rock fragments where toolworkers shaped points with hammerstones; slight evidence, but enough to demonstrate that man has been in the Rockies twenty to thirty centuries longer than previously suspected. Geologists have tracked the great glaciers of the Pleistocene which began to recede some one hundred and twenty centuries ago. Few animals lived in the mountains when the great ice filled the valleys. But as soon as larger animals recolonized the Rockies, man came hunting.

The landscape probably looked much like the region two or three kilometres from the toe of North America's most familiar glacier, the Athabasca tongue of the Columbia Icefield where it descends from the Park Range to the Icefields Parkway. Some trees—alpine fir, whitebark pine, small aspen and willows—and mats of grass had taken root in the thin soil. Other species of mammals likely inhabited the slopes: a larger species of sheep related to the bighorn, mountain goats, caribou, marmots, rabbits, and ground squirrels; and predators who lived on them: cougars, wolves, wolverines, foxes, bears, lynx. In the late Pleistocene many species of mammals disappeared from North America—the North American elephants, the giant bison, the giant moose, the giant beaver, the large Pleistocene sheep, the camelid—probably because a new predator, man, had intruded upon the American landscape. Few identifiable fragments of the hunters' prey in the Rockies remain, but in a hundred centuries neither animals nor the men who hunt them have changed.

The first North Americans clothed themselves in garb made of hides sewn with sinew. Long before they reached the southern Rockies, experience had taught them to turn the hides inside out, the fur inside for warmth and insulation. For generations these people had lived in the realms of winter and ice. Survival informed every aspect of their lives. If they left clothing behind when they returned to the foothills, it cannot have survived. Made of hides, it rotted within decades, leaving no trace. One bone bead is the solitary testament to their concepts of decoration and clothing.

What circumstance brought these people to the base of the mountain now called Mount Cory, where they, like Banff's residents and visitors today, could gaze at Mount Bourgeau and Sulphur Mountain? The glacial history of the northern hemisphere provides some answers. In the last great advance of the continental glaciers the ice spread from the cooler highland centres. From the high mountains of North America's western rim, the Cordilleran Ice Sheet spread westward to the Pacific Ocean, riding over Vancouver Island in the process; it also spilled eastward down great valleys into the region now called Alberta. A second sheet, far deeper and more massive than the Cordilleran Sheet, grew from centres in the intensely cold climate of the continental interior, coalescing into the Keewatin Sheet. Ice, a fluid, acts like water: it seeks its own height. The ice of the continental sheet did not flow uphill, but as its depth increased to a level of 1,500 metres it mounted the Canadian

Shield and fanned out for a hundred centuries, its waves of ice finally lapping on the foothills of the Rockies. Like a slow tide of molasses, the ice spread, engulfing ever-higher landscapes as it overtook the altitude of the long slope from Hudson Bay to the base of the Rockies.

Along a line east of—but parallel to—the ridge of the Rockies the advancing sheets of ice met, later diverging there in the long centuries of the thaw. As winds from the Pacific today pass over the Rockies, becoming chinooks when they descend to the eastern valleys and the foothills, warm dry winds that exhilarate winterbound spirits, so they have done for millennia. The late Pleistocene chinooks drove the ice back before them. The two sheets retreated toward their centres. Along the foothills of the Rockies the melting exposed a corridor of land where animals and people travelled freely for the first time in a hundred centuries.

Archaeologists argue about the oldest evidence of man in the New World. Scientists have carbon-dated some sites in the Yukon in the Old Crow Basin at three hundred centuries, but few other indisputable pieces of evidence predate the retreat of the ice sheets. The storage of water in the continental ice sheets lowered the level of the oceans, exposing a land bridge for the peoples of eastern Asia to journey east to the Yukon Valley and into northern North America. The migration into the Americas may have occurred after the growth of the continental ice sheets had lowered the seas to expose the land bridge, yet before the sheets merged to barricade the land route to southern North America. If the wanderers arrived before the coalescing ice sealed the route south, they made their way south in the lee of the Rockies to the plains and deserts of the American interior, then on to Central and South America while the ice sealed their route behind them in Canada, erasing the record of their chill passage. More people then arrived after the ice barrier developed, while the land bridge—several times wider than the Isthmus of Panama—connected North America and Asia.

Later, after the ice sheets melted and the oceans rose to inundate the land bridge and reform the Bering Strait, more people arrived in America, this time by boat. The Aleutian Islands enabled the later American pioneers, forebears of the Inuit and the Aleuts, to island-hop to the New World in pursuit of fish and seals. Without deliberation, pursuing neither dreams nor wealth nor opportunity, all the first Americans sought survival.

The Inuit and the Aleuts bear little resemblance to their forerunners in North America. Evidence points to an origin for both Amerindians and Inuit in Asia, the Asiatic features of the latter indicating their more recent arrival. In likelihood no one shall ever identify the Indians' racial forebears. The passage of a hundred to two hundred centuries has erased most elements of their Asian background.

In North America no ice blocked the migrants' eastward route up the interior valley of the Yukon River and down the Porcupine River to the Old

Crow region in the Yukon and the Mackenzie River's delta. Not until they had advanced thousands of kilometres inland, generations after their ancestors first reached the continent, did the people come up against the ice. They did not think of it as a barrier to their way south. In their ignorance of maps, they knew no south. They knew only their own terrain, but they knew it in nerve, fibre, sinew, mind, and every perception.

In the slow centuries when the continental ice sheets melted, plants from the northern refuges moved south as sun and warm winds bared the glacially-scoured land. Northern mammals like the caribou, the moose, the giant moose, bison, giant bison, camelids, woolly mammoths, mastodons, musk-oxen, sought the new pastures growing southward. Their predators followed them. Man—a predator—followed the herds. As the corridor opened northward, other mammals—sheep, deer, and goats—moved north. The poet Earle Birney, in a striking phrase, calls the isthmus of land between the oceans of ice the "Mammoth Corridors."

Generation by generation, advancing ten to fifty or sixty kilometres in a lifespan, the hunter-gatherers followed the animals' trails in the great river valley, the course of the ancient Mackenzie and Athabasca flows. We cannot name these people by their tribes; the languages they spoke—a usual means of definition of tribes—are more remote from today's languages than English is from Sanskrit. Those pioneers a hundred centuries ago spoke a language long forgotten, much modified, never written. The first travellers in the Rockies, precursors of today's American Indians, were not likely ancestors of the people who inhabit the Rockies today. The descendants of the precursors may now dwell in Argentina or Tennessee, the Caribbean or Manitoba.

Where the transverse valleys of the Athabasca, the Saskatchewan, the Bow, and the Oldman rivers descend from the mountains to the plains, the glaciers melted first. There the land was lower and warmer. Animals that had retreated south, like the bison, moved north and into the mountains where they found the grasses they'd grown habituated to. They quickly repopulated the mountain valleys upon the ice's melting and the growth of plant cover. The wandering peoples, ever hungry, sought them out.

A band of toolmaking hunters entered the Rockies 11,500 years ago. On the south-facing slope of the Bow Valley, at the shore of the glacial lake, they made camp long enough to find flaking rocks to form edged tools for killing and fleshing animals and for butchering the meat. They cured the hides, made clothing and tents, perhaps found moments to relax in the warm summer sun. The ashes of their ancient hearth rested on the soil. After they departed, a storm dislodged a slurry of mud and gravel on the slope above their camp, washing it down from the slope above, forty to fifty centimetres in a single spill, sealing the evidence of their visit. The Paleo-Indians left traces of man's first passage in the Rockies 6,000 years before the Egyptians left their records in tombs and pyramids.

In the centuries to come other bands followed their route, keeping to the lake's north side where the sun first melted the snow cover in the thin forest. The logic of the first campsite prevailed. Those who came later camped in the same place. Mud and gravel from the slope above concealed the testament of their campsites too. So it continued for thousands of years. The outlet stream eventually carved a passage between Tunnel Mountain and Mount Rundle, and the lake receded from the shoreline campsite.

An archaeological team, slowly and carefully exposing the site in the summer of 1983, found deposit upon deposit of silt and tephra—ash exploded from the volcanoes of the Cascades near the mouth of the Columbia River and borne inland by wind. Since tephra indicates geological events of known date, it aids dating profiles in the soil. But, more meaningful than the deposits of soil, the team discovered seven separate layers with evidence of human habitation over a period of 10,000 years.

What led the archaeologists to what they call the Vermilion Lakes site? Its logical features: good protection; water nearby; the shelter from the prevailing wind the slope to the west affords; and level land, an aspect of real estate rare in mountain environments. One other factor imposed the selection: the site lay by the route proposed for highway twinning; construction would disturb, obliterate, or bury deeper the record the soil had concealed and protected. Shallow test holes along the route every twenty metres in nearly every case revealed evidence of earlier human presence. In some cases surface exposures from previous road cuts, stream erosion, even gopher holes, revealed tool flakes. As it proceeds west up the Bow Valley, the Trans-Canada Highway follows a trail of the ages.

Gross testing with a backhoe revealed the potential richness of the region. Then, test hole by test hole, the archaeologists proceeded to the Vermilion Lakes site, one of five sites they explored in greater depth beside the proposed highway development. The others were fruitful, but the Vermilion Lakes site —EhPv-8 in the archaeologists' designation—yielded one of the oldest records of man in southwestern Canada.

Distinguishing three major silt layers as they excavated the site, the field workers found evidence of occupation over a period of 7,000 years in the highest layer—the top twenty to twenty-five centimetres—including items from the culture of the Tobacco Plains People. (Archaeologists avoid labelling evidence from prehistorical societies with the names of extant groups. The Tobacco Plains in northern Montana were the home of a people who made similar artifacts. They are today the home of the Kootenay Indians. The Tobacco Plains People may have been the ancestors of the Kootenay; more likely they were a different group who earlier lived in the same region.)

Dated 5,000 to 7,500 years before the present (B.P.), ten projectile points of the Bitterroot type, made for throwing with an atlatl, a throwing stick the hunter can grasp in his hand to increase both the speed and accuracy of his projectile, lay in the lower level of the highest silt unit. (North American archaeologists who concentrate on the western half of the continent use a system of diagnostic projectile points for dating cultural periods. The style and shape of projectile points and hand-shaped stone tools are similar throughout western North America for long—and datable—cultural periods. Points of the Avonlea phase, for example, are small side-notched arrow points made 1,000 to 1,800 years ago. Tobacco Plains-type points—arrowheads—in the following phase, more crudely and swiftly made, show inefficient use of the stone the toolmakers employed.)

From the middle silt layer the diggers recovered two projectile points, similar in fashioning to two other point styles (Plains-Mountains and Agate Basin complexes) which date between 8,000 and 10,500 years old. They estimated they'd reached 9,500 years into the past in their digging. Still they dug deeper.

In the deepest silt unit the archaeologists found several stone artifacts and hundreds of chips and flakes. The ancient camp had been a paleolithic factory where toolmakers cracked boulders down to usable sizes, and repaired tools for re-use. Carbon dating of charcoal fragments in the stratum established the campsite's age at approximately 11,000 years B.P. In the stratum immediately above the toolworking camp the team found large quantities of charcoal in a camp it believes was a butchering site because of the many fragments of caribou, sheep, moose, and rabbit bones. Carbon dating of the higher—hence usually more recent—camp established its age as approximately 600 years older than the deeper layer. The archaeological team concluded that a landslide or flood had mingled the charcoal, placing the older material above the younger, creating the puzzling sequence. The scientists found no projectile points in the lowest stratum to aid them in dating the site. Upon the completion of the excavation, they refilled the pit they had so carefully examined.

The delicacy and the importance of the site to the prehistory of western Canada provide a reminder that amateur archaeologizing can easily destroy evidence of earlier cultures. Amateurs can disrupt irreplaceable evidence, and the fines are severe ($50,000 maximum) and justifiable.

The Bow Valley Trail's history compares with that of the other great trails of the ages. Fourteen years before the Vermilion Lakes dig, a University of Calgary archaeological team located sites and artifacts exposed by erosion throughout the Bow and Cascade valleys and elsewhere in Banff National Park. That team suspected human life in the central Rockies antedated the usual speculation by thousands of years, but it lacked the funds and the time to discover what the Vermilion Lakes team unearthed in 1983.

An archaeological team working in 1980 in the Sibbald Flat region of Sibbald Creek, west of Calgary and south of the Trans-Canada Highway near Moose Mountain in the foothills, about eleven kilometres from the Front Range of the Rockies, found thousands of artifacts dating over an

11,000-year period, including the first artifacts found in Alberta of the Fluted Point Tradition. Another proposed highway routing provoked the Sibbald Creek dig. In the shallowest portions of their excavation the scientists found numerous samples of animal remains. The site, they surmise, had been an autumn and early winter hunting camp for both Plains and Rocky Mountain Indians for the past thousand years.

Archaeologists in the years to come may refine the ancient history of the Rockies, but whatever they discover, they know they'll be unable to extend the record further back. Inevitably they reach a level where the Pleistocene ice erased the record if it ever existed. But they now know that since people arrived in the Rockies about a hundred and fifteen centuries ago, the mountain valleys have been busy.

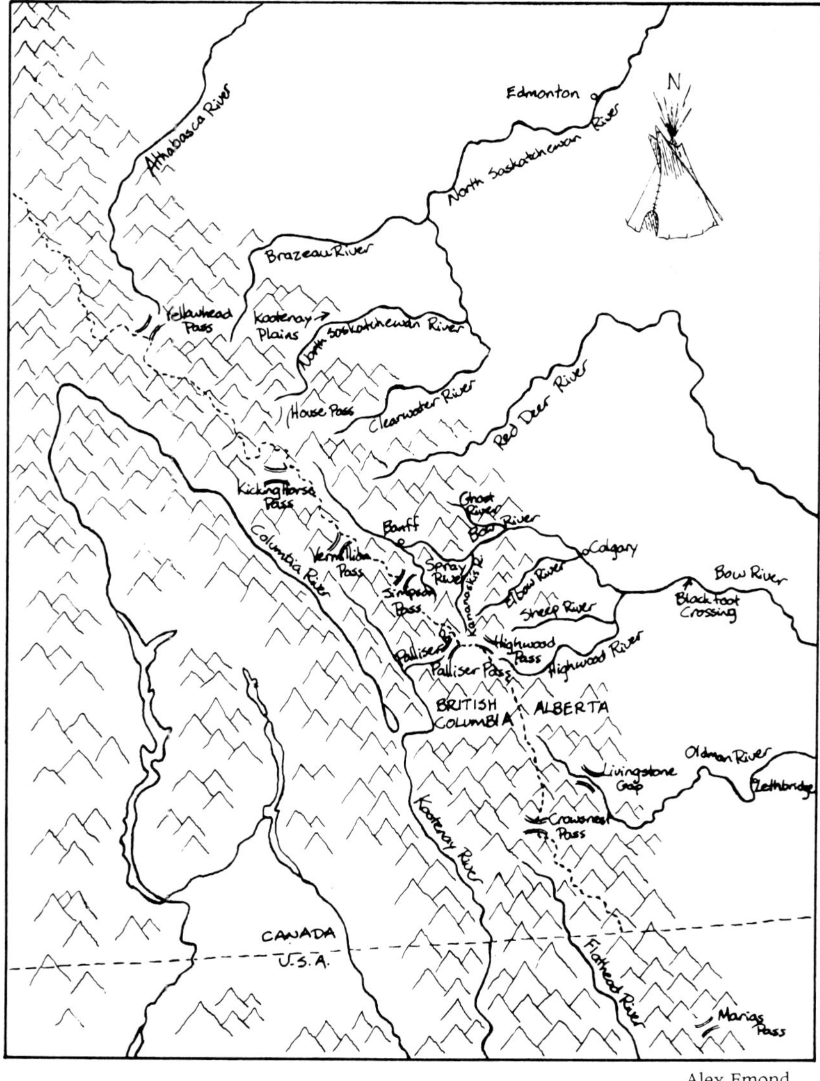

Alex Emond

2

The Mountain Peoples

The Great Spirit created a human being from the Earth. When he came alive the being was burnt, dark-like. So the Great Spirit tried another one, and set it out in the sun further north, another image, and when it came to life, it was pale. So the Great Spirit tried another one, and when it came to life it was brown. The Great Spirit moved the black people to a hot country. He moved the pale people to a country with a cooler climate. He kept the brown people in that place where he had created them all.

George McLean, Medicine Man of the Stoneys, 1964

The Canadian Rockies, a smaller range of mountains than their reputation suggests, with the American Rockies, their extension in the United States, form the ridgepole of North America. But Canada's Rockies, spectacular in the boldness of glacially scoured rock and crowned with glaciers, rarely attain the height of the Interior Ranges of British Columbia to the west of them or the American Rockies. Contrast enhances their grandeur: from prairie or parkland, the Rockies seem an awesome barrier.

Three parallel sets of ranges define them. On the east stand the Front Ranges, the lower, usually grey, limestone peaks in which the strata typically lie at an angle to the horizon. In the middle loom the Main Ranges, quartzite and dolomite peaks nearly 4,000 metres high that bear most of the Rockies' glaciers and the lakes and rivers they give birth to. To the west are the Western Ranges, lower mountains again, frequently rounded by glaciation during the Pleistocene. The distance from the foothills in Alberta to the Rocky Mountain Trench in British Columbia—the width of the combined ranges—is approximately 200 kilometres. The valleys in the Rockies usually parallel the ranges—generally southeast to northwest—but transverse valleys intersect all three ranges, spilling rivers to the prairies on the east, to the Rocky Mountain Trench on the west.

Glacially fed rivers drop rapidly from the summits through thickly forested valleys that were the wanderers' usual routes in the Rockies through the ages. As altitude increases, the forests thin. In the highest vegetated regions the forest becomes sparse and miniaturized. Moving from one valley to another, residents of the Rockies often trekked upslope to alpine passes where it was difficult both to find protection against the harsh high winds and to find food where animals other than sheep and goats are rare. The nomadic peoples could cross the passes only in summer or autumn. Given the seasonal restrictions, the Rockies—like most other mountain ranges—restricted easy movement.

A hundred and more centuries passed. The first Americans fanned out, populating both Americas. People adapted to different habitats. Their languages spread and changed. The centuries, despite archaeological finds like the Vermilion Lakes site, keep their secrets. In 1969 an archaeological team working in Banff National Park located forty-eight sites in the Bow Valley, thirteen in the North Saskatchewan-Howse Pass region, fifty-four sites along the Cascade River, five on the Red Deer River, and two sites on the Clearwater, sites ranging from the valley floor to one alpine hunting camp, on Corral Creek below Boulder Pass, and to the mountains' high ridges. They found butchering camps, flint-knapping sites, diagnostic points, and, near the Hoodoos, a mollusc shell band. The archaeologists concluded both Plains and Plateau Peoples resided in the region the park now occupies.

In 1970 a similar team working in Jasper National Park and the Ya-Ha-Tinda Ranch on Banff National Park's eastern boundary along the Red Deer River located many more sites. They found the Athabasca Valley had fewer sites than the Bow Valley: of twenty-two sites found in Jasper Park, nine were from the period after native contact with white men. The team concluded the Jasper region held little importance for prehistoric groups. In the Ya-Ha-Tinda (a Stoney phrase meaning Meadow in the Mountains) they located forty-nine prehistoric sites, two of them early prehistoric, and believed prehistoric groups probably inhabited the valley for many winters. The Meadow in the Mountains in prehistoric times likely provided winter range for bison, and more recently for elk.

Four centuries ago voices rise loud enough for memory to hold them. The peoples who lived in and near the Rockies start bearing their familiar tribal designations.

For the hundred centuries after the continental ice sheets dwindled, the Rockies supported life marginally. To the east, on the prairies and in the foothills, roved the bison millions upon which the Plains Indians depended. Life posed difficulties in the boreal forest, but the food pyramids stood on larger bases than in the Rockies where fewer animals roamed, and the terrain made pursuit difficult. Only the poorest people, driven to the edges of other societies, sought survival in the Rockies' meagre, demanding circumstance.

Few people lived anywhere in most of North America, but fewer lived in the region where the Rockies dwindle to lower peaks and the Peace River carves its eastward-flowing route through them. In the eighteenth century a new force would oblige the migration of the Déné-speaking Western Beaver Indians from the lower Peace River drainage into the Rockies of the area. On the west-draining slopes of the same region lived Interior Salish people, the Shuswap, who subsisted in northern British Columbia's difficult terrain.

In the Rockies along the Athabasca River on the eastern slope dwelt the Woodland Peoples, Déné tribes happiest in stream and forest country. West of them, on both sides of Yellowhead Pass, more Shuswap lived in the dense cordilleran forests and on their game and on the salmon that swam upstream from the Pacific to the western marches of the Rockies. Summers the Shuswap lived in tepee-like tents; winters in pit dwellings with pole roofs chinked with moss and covered with mud, entering by a stripped spar ladder protruding through the smoke hole. An archaeologist investigated fourteen such pit-house remnants near the Banff Springs Golf Course in the 1920s. In recent decades golf course employees have filled them in—because they posed hazards to golf carts, thereby assuring their protection. Some archaeologists, considering the Shuswap or Shuswap-like dwellings near Banff to be anomalies, believe they signify a Shuswap experiment in living in the Rockies that failed.

In the central Rockies, near the headwaters of the North Saskatchewan and Bow Rivers, and along the Kootenay and Columbia Rivers, the Kootenay People lived on both sides of the Great Divide. A small nation with no kin in the plains or woodland region, their language related to the Uto-Aztecan languages of Mexico, the Kootenay lived in the foothills and upper plains for centuries before they migrated across the divide.

The Kootenay crossed the Rockies frequently, west to the warmer valleys of the Columbia and Kootenay Rivers for springs and summers when they practised agrarian lives, growing corn and tobacco, engaging in fishing, east to the foothills and the prairies for bison hunts in autumn and winter when the bison retreated to the wooded hills for protection from the northern gales. Four centuries ago, they undoubtedly resided in the Rockies, not merely as passers-by but as permanent residents. Game populations in the mountains would not equal those of the prairies, but they would have been more than sufficient for small family groups. For their plains excursions the Kootenay still used the tepees, but they may have adapted Shuswap architecture for the pit dwellings of Banff. In 1811, the fur trader Alexander Henry the Younger, investigating the Clearwater River, a tributary of the North Saskatchewan River, noted "the remains of some of the dwellings of the Kootenays, built of wood, straw and pine branches." He had seen similar dwellings "along Rivière de la Jolie Prairie and Ram River," and concluded that "this gives us every reason to suppose that nation formerly dwelt along the foot of these mountains, and even as far as our present establishment [Rocky Mountain House], near which the remains of their lodges are still to be seen." The ethnologist Claude E. Schaeffer distinguishes a group he calls the Michel Prairie Kutenai who lived in the Crowsnest Pass region and south to the Waterton Lakes.

In the southern Canadian Rockies, near the headwaters of the Milk and Oldman Rivers, the Snakes, a Shoshone-speaking people, lived on the fringes of the Blackfoot Nation of the great plains. In contact with other people of the interior valleys of the American west, the Snakes would be the first tribe in the Northern Rockies to obtain the horse.

These various peoples were never confined to one habitat over the centuries. The Shoshone who dwell now in the Great Basin of the western United States developed divers means to live wherever they moved. In the Canadian Rockies they fashioned lives appropriate to circumstance. Local conditions obliged the northern Kootenay to adapt different living techniques when they became transmontane people. In the valleys to the west of the Rockies they found others of their farflung linguistic group who had for generations derived part of their subsistence as fishermen.

America's first peoples did not live isolated from each other, fearful of any other tribe's approach. Like many societies, some Indian nations sustain themselves on fables of their warrior qualities, their prowess in battle, not upon their well-managed harmony with the land or the richness of their culture, religion, or costume. Well-developed trails and trade routes criss-crossed the Rockies: peoples who had items other people wanted traded them for what they wanted. Obsidian from the Yellowstone River area makes splendid arrowheads, tools easily formed to a razor-sharp edge. Yellowstone obsidian shows up all over western North America, and in such profusion trade must have dispersed it, not raids or the casual re-use of arrowheads picked up from spent arrows. Many people prized Catlinite, a carvable red-coloured stone found only in one place in Minnesota, because they could shape it into pipes; the Indians dispersed it and another material, grey-green dolomitic pipestone, throughout the plains and mountains. Shells from the Pacific Ocean show up at locations far from the sea, among other artifacts of inland dwellers who prized the shells. Other shells from the Gulf of Mexico reached the Déné of northern Alberta and the Northwest Territories. Ochre from Vermilion Pass in the central Canadian Rockies reached the prairies and the woodlands for use as body paint. The peoples of other regions desired the medicinal remedies the Cree developed from plants of the northern forest. Other tribes valued the Mountain Stoneys' pharmacology—which they probably developed when they travelled westward along the woodland fringe with the Cree. The story of trade among the Indians of western North America before the onset of the fur trade is speculative, but evidence abounds to show most tribes traded more amicably than their narratives often suggest.

Four hundred years ago the scattered peoples of the Rockies felt new forces which disrupted the harmony with their plains neighbours to the east. In the following century ripples from stones dropped afar washed into their lives. Something different, threatening, combative began affecting the lives and traditions of the Mountain Peoples.

English entrepreneurs began developing a fur-trading empire centred on Hudson Bay in the woodland interior of North America, skirting the French fur-trading empire in the St Lawrence River and Lake Champlain regions. The Hudson's Bay Company—The Company of Adventurers of England Trading into Hudson's Bay is its grandiloquent seventeenth-century name—obtained in 1670, from King Charles II, who had no claim to it but nevertheless granted it, a monopoly in the fur trade in all lands draining into Hudson Bay.

Without the cordiality, aid, and co-operation of the Indian peoples, the venture would have ended in fiasco. For twenty years the company huddled on the shore of the great inland sea, enticing the natives to bring their furs down the Nelson River to their fort on Hudson Bay. But the Company's trade required penetrating the continental interior. In 1690, guided by the Cree whose language he had learned, the young Henry Kelsey departed the fort for a sojourn of a year and a half in what he called The Inland Country of Good Report, a name he coined from its Cree designation.

The young man's party travelled upriver into the continental interior, where Kelsey wrote the first poem in English from western Canada. In his poem and journal he describes the land, the traditions and the ways of its peoples. His notes locate the Stoney People, the Assiniboine in southern Manitoba, some of whom would reside in the Canadian Rockies a century later. To benefit the company he worked for, Kelsey temporarily effected a peace between the Cree and the Assiniboine.

Canada's east- and west-running rivers create its geographic integrity. Of the greatest rivers all but one run east and west. The exception is the Mackenzie. All but one rise in the Rockies. The exception is the St Lawrence. The rivers provide the key to the fur trade's development. In the early seventeenth century French entrepreneurs developed trapping and trading in the St Lawrence drainage and the Lake Champlain region. Gunpowder came to the tribes living around Lake Superior when the Great Lakes became part of the French Empire. Its force would affect the peoples of the Rockies within a century. In their search for new fur-bearing regions, fur traders inevitably proceeded west on the rivers.

On the wooded edges of the Canadian Shield in the Lake of the Woods region, a nation of people set out on a wandering migration, eventually affecting all the Mountain Peoples.

The wanderers were the Stoney or the Assiniboine—part of the Sioux Nation, those who speak dialects of the Sioux language. The names their foes gave them frequently distinguish Indian tribes and bands. The Stoney call themselves the Nakodah—the people. The Cree, noting the Nakodah cooked their food by dropping heated stones into birchbark vessels or by placing it on heated boulders, called them the Stone Cookers, the Stone-cooking people, Assine-boets or, in Kelsey's words, the Mountain Poets. Time shortened the nickname to Stoney. Nakodah is cognate with Dakota in other dialects, familiar in the names of two American states.

In their westward movements, the Stoney split into three or more bands. The Chinikis reached the western mountains first, and have lived in the Rockies so long they say they "have always lived here." By the mid-eighteenth century, if not sooner, some Stoney were crossing the mountains for war raids and to capture horses and slaves. Later accounts verify their knowledge of the Rockies, their ability to live comfortably in mountains. Other Stoney bands travelled the northern edges of the prairies and plains, moving into the woodland and parkland frontier, living on the bison economy of the plains, but aware of the fur-bearing animal country of the lake and river habitats. Another band, people who now call themselves the Bearspaws, travelled a more southern route, protected for a period by the Blackfoot. Not until the late eighteenth century did most of the Stoney reach the foothills where they remained; not until a century after that did the bands converge again.

What force impelled the Stoney migration? A scarcity of food perhaps, or a desire to set out for new worlds. In all likelihood the fur trade in the Great Lakes region created opportunities for other Indians who may have forced the Stoneys to seek a new land. A Stoney chief in the early twentieth century recalled his tribe's traditions for the migration:

> Old Hector Crawler....told how the Indians had come to the mountains from the 'Nakotas,' not Dakota as we call it....The Indians who lived on the plains or prairies had a great sickness about four hundred years ago. Hector called it a kind of flu, but his son-in-law George McLean said it was smallpox. Many died, whole tepees of people. (They speak of a family as a tepee of Indians.) Sometimes there would be just one boy or one girl left in each tepee, and the Indians tried to get away from this great sickness and went off in different directions, but still the sickness went with them and many died. The Stoneys came to the mountains and the sickness gradually left them.
>
> Catharine Whyte, letter to her mother, February 28, 1945.

A greater force than the Stoney migration was already affecting the residents of the Rockies: what the Peigans called big dogs, the horses the Spaniards introduced to the Americas. Horses quickly became an ally of the western Indian peoples—beasts of burden, means of swift transport, token of wealth, source of sport and recreation. Early in the seventeenth century, the horse reached the upper Kootenay and Columbia valleys and the Kootenay and Snake Indians by the interior valleys of the western cordillera. By the late eighteenth century wild horses were abundant in the Rocky Mountain Trench, though the Kootenays were not adept at securing many of them for their own purposes or to trade. From them the Plains People, by raid or by trade, obtained the horse. No longer would dogs haul heavy hide tepees on travois; a single horse could carry the burden.

Their traditional foe now equipped with horses and arms, Kootenay sentinels from the shelter of poplar copses observed scouts of the Plains People riding the big dogs. They observed the rapid pursuit of the bison, watched riders run down prey, spearing and injuring it as their horses overtook the lumbering, dust-raising bison. A man on foot would fall easily to an enemy on a horse. Cautious people, the Kootenay fled to the mountains to avoid conflict with the Plains People. Holding council among themselves, deciding more caution would govern their movements, they retreated farther west.

Along the eastern frontier of the Rockies two north-south routes sustained a trail of the ages, the "Mammoth Corridors." On the prairie ran the Great North Trail of the Blackfoot Nation, from the Missouri River's northern frontier to the wooded edges of the Battle River south of Edmonton. West of it, in the foothills and the Front Ranges of the Rockies, people fearful of the Plains People struck a parallel route. Its origin, like that of the Great North Trail, probably lies in antiquity, centuries before the Snakes, Shuswap, Kootenay, and Stoney followed its concealed route. From the foothills trail, hunters descended to the plains by the North Saskatchewan, Red Deer, Bow, Elbow, Highwood, Oldman, and Crowsnest Rivers.

The Blackfoot believed Napi or Old Man, the trickster god and creator of the world, had played at bowls with the animals of creation, at the "Old Man's playing field," a level field near Livingstone Gap. Napi, according to legend, lost the game, but when storms raise thunderheads over the foothills, and echoes of thunder growl and rebound against the mountains, they say the Old Man is bowling again. Where the Oldman River, named for Napi, breaches the Front Ranges, the same field marked the frontier of contending nations where competition reconciled rivalries in an Indian Olympics. As lacrosse substituted for war among the Woodland Peoples of the east, the sport of the Old Man's gaming field allowed expression of hostility in a manner short of mayhem. Eleven cairns about thirty-five centimetres high defined the playing field. In late 1792 a band of Peigan headed south from the Bow River to meet a group of Kootenays who'd brought horses over the mountains to trade. Peter Fidler, a Hudson's Bay Company fur trader and surveyor travelling with the Peigan, describes the game in his journal entry for December 31, 1792. The game demanded its players dart an arrow through a small rolling hoop, ten centimetres in diameter: "those that put the arrow within the hoop while rolling along is reckoned to have gamed." The Mountain People, whose stalking of wary game with bow and arrow in forests required greater accuracy, and who would later demonstrate better marksmanship with rifles, likely won most competitions. Fidler says the Indians gave him a "surprising & ridiculas" account of the game's origin. They told him a white man from the south, "many ages ago," introduced the game to them to "bury all anamosities betwixt the Different Tribes—by assembling here—& playing together—They also say that this same person made the Buffalo—on purpose for the Indians. They describe him as a very old white bearded man & several things very ridiculous." A similar game, called Hoop and Pole, exists in most Amerindian cultures, and several American museums preserve examples of the hoop from the Peigan bands of southern Alberta. Paul Kane, travelling west of the mountains in the 1840s, sketched and later painted Plateau Indians playing the game in what is now eastern Washington.

Fidler hoped to bring the Kootenay into the Company's expanding fur trade, though the Blackfoot opposed any expansion of trade to the tribe with which they had an uneasy alliance. The Kootenay told Fidler their home was five days west of where he and the Peigan met them. The Kootenay (Fidler spells it Cottanahau among other ways) would accept nearly anything—old hatchets, old kettles—in trade for their own hard-caught horses. The Kootenay camped in tepees smaller than those of the Plains Indians. Fidler describes another sort of shelter the Kootenay made by taking a copse of aspens, which, "with their [hand] ax they notched the trees all on the out side, forming a circle the size of the tents. Then bent all the tops together & put on the Tents—this was very expeditiously done." Fidler describes their basketry utensils made of "the inner bark of the Pine—some of them are made of Pine roots—others of Grass—made in a very neat manner & water tight," and says:

> ...they have several curious shapes of these culenary utensils—some being made exactly in the form of a Tea Kettle wanting the Neck—in there they boil their provisions...by immersing hot stones into it—& boiling it in that Manner—The Implement they have for getting wood consists of a red Deer's horn all the branches being broken off except the long one next the head. This is sharpened like a chissel by rubbing it upon stones—& this constitutes their hatchet—They have also wedges made of the same materials with a Stone fixed in a [?] as a handle—with these they were very soon cut down a Tree & split or rive it into smaller pieces fit for firewood—this I saw them perform with expeditious success. Their arrows are considerably longer than any of the Different [Plains?] Tribes—& shod with flint.

The fur trader also describes the fishing talents of the Kootenay, indicating they held a region to the north of the Bow River as especially fine. They were probably speaking of Lake Minnewanka near Banff, but the geography is uncertain. The Kootenay told Fidler no bison lived in one valley due west of Devil's Head (prominent black knot of a mountain north of and visible from the Bow Valley), but elk and deer provided food for the small family hunting groups. A sign language name for the Tobacco Plains Kootenay employs the symbol for the white-tailed deer. Fidler reports "the rivers on that side are well stocked with fish of which those several tribes who inhabit those parts are fond of & eat a great deal of them—Sturgeon is also found."

The fire history of the Bow Valley throws interesting light on the history of the early inhabitants of the Rockies. Research upsets the image of the valleys of the Rockies before the arrival of the railroad as thick virgin forest stretching from the foothills to the Columbia Valley. Dense forests result from the National Parks' fire suppression techniques. In earlier centuries fires broke out frequently, depleting the fuel burden regularly, resulting in less damage by the big scorchers, but advantageously opening up range land for ungulates. The Déné of northern Alberta still use forest and grass fires to create range for browsing species, and the Kootenay Indians of northern Montana have similar traditions. Resident in the Canadian Rockies, the Kootenay may have practised the same techniques. Mountain Peoples didn't start fires wantonly. They were creating range for the animals their lives depended upon, and keeping routes open for trail and transport purposes. Setting fires at regular intervals kept the fires small, rarely getting out of hand and crowning out, keeping the understory clear of down timber and deadfall. Fire historians are not certain that forest fire patterns in the Canadian Rockies reflect the influence of man, but the more data they gather the more it seems likely.

The northern Plains People quickly became horsemen, and the horse transformed their economy. Hunting bison had been an arduous, time-consuming task, involving skill and caution in selecting a site where men and women drove the great beasts over a cliff. On horses, as the Kootenay had observed, hunters raced as fleetly as their prey. No longer did subsistence shape their lives. The hunters killed relatively easily, and luxury—of a sort—entered the lives of the Plains People. The horse enhanced mobility and a band could carry more possessions. Time became the greatest luxury: time for leisure and artistic expression, time for wandering, time and the compulsion to engage in the great innovative sport of the plains, horse-rustling.

The hunters followed the herds, and the people moved readily from regions of shortage to areas of abundance. The horse's influence likely made Plains People more bellicose, if only because more mobile tribes encountered each other more frequently. Expanding the territory they hunted in, the Plains Indians drove the Kootenay over the Rockies permanently, the Kootenay displacing the Shoshone who lived there before them. The horse influenced the lives of the Woodland People far less; in deep forest and swampy country it served few purposes.

In the forest frontier the fur trade more significantly altered Indian life. The Woodland People reaped rewards from European forays into North America: trade goods like copper and iron pots and kettles, needles and awls, flints and steels; decorative items like beads; axeheads and other tools like snare wire for trapping, and weapons, guns among them. All these things the fur trade introduced to the Canadian west.

Henry Kelsey undertook his journey of 1690-92 to persuade the inland Indians they'd benefit by bringing pelts downstream to the Hudson's Bay Company fort on Hudson Bay. In trade they'd obtain cooking vessels, guns, blankets, axes and other metal objects. Nations of people, stone age in their technology, readily adopted the imported technology. The Company had no intention of civilizing the natives, but it used every means to assure a constant supply of furs. Economic advantages to the Indians were immediate, hence those who lived nearer the fort thwarted the efforts of the inland Indians to obtain the new weapons and resources the fur trade introduced.

Scourge struck the Plains and Mountain Peoples in the early 1770s. The pestilence of smallpox spread among them, felling man, woman, and child, ''as the fire consumes the dry grass of the field,'' according to the fur trader Alexander Mackenzie, who grimly depicted the disease's effects:

> The fatal infection spread around with a painful rapidity which no flight could escape, and with a fatal effect that nothing could resist. It destroyed with its pestilential breath whole families and tribes; and the horrid scene presented to those who had the melancholy and afflicting opportunity of beholding it, a combination of the dead, the dying, and such as to avoid the horrid fate of their friends around them, prepared to disappoint the plague of its prey, by terminating their own existence.
>
> The habits and lives of these devoted people, which provided not to-day for the wants of to-morrow, must have heightened the pains of such an affliction, by leaving them not only without remedy, but even without alleviation. Nought was left them but to submit in agony and despair.
>
> To aggravate the picture, if aggravation were possible, may be added, the putrid carcases which the wolves, with a furious voracity, dragged forth from the huts, or which were mangled within them by dogs, whose hunger was satisfied with the disfigured remains of their masters. Nor was it uncommon for the father of a family, whom the affection had not reached, to call them around him, to represent the cruel sufferings and horrid fate of their relations, from the influence of some evil spirit who was preparing to extirpate their race; and to incite them to baffle death, with all its horrors, by their own poniards. At the same time, if their hearts failed them in this necessary act, he was himself ready to perform the deed of mercy with his own hand, as the last act of his affection, and instantly to follow them to the common place of rest and refuge from human evil.

David Thompson, whose career in the fur trade overlaps Mackenzie's, estimates three out of every five Indians in western Canada died in the smallpox epidemics:

> More Men died in proportion than Women and Children, for unable to bear the heat of the fever they rushed into the Rivers and Lakes to cool themselves, and the greater part thus perished. The countries were in a manner depopulated, the Natives allowed that far more than one half had died; ...despair and despondency had to give way to active hunting both for provisions, clothing and all the necessaries of life, for in their sickness, as usual, they had offered allmost every thing they had to the Good Spirit and to the Bad, to preserve their lives, and were in a manner destitute of everything.

Throughout the western plains and mountains smallpox swept horrifically. The old man Saukamappee, a Cree by birth whom the Peigans had kidnapped in his childhood, said: ''Death came over us all, and swept away more than half of us by the Small pox, of which we knew nothing until it brought death among us. We caught it from the Snake Indians.'' His grim tale equals Mackenzie's account:

> Our Scouts were out for our security, when some returned and informed us of a considerable camp which was too large to attack and something very suspicious about it; from a high knowl they had a good view of the camp, but saw none of the men hunting, or going about....Next morning at the dawn of day, we attacked the Tents, and with our sharp flat daggers and knives, cut through the tents and entered for the fight; but our war whoop instantly stopt, our eyes were appalled with terror; there was no one to fight with but the dead and the dying, each a mass of corruption. We did not touch them, but left the tents, and held a council on what was to be done. We all thought the Bad Spirit had made himself master of the camp and destroyed them. It was agreed to take some of the best of the tents, and any other plunder that was clean and good, which we did, and also took away the few Horses they had, and returned to our camp.
>
> The second day after this dreadful disease broke out in our camp, and spread from one tent to another as if the Bad Spirit carried it. We had no belief that one Man could give it to another, any more than a wounded Man could give his wound to another.

Saukamappee's words reveal the bitterness of tribal xenophobia. Smallpox, introduced by Europeans, may have arrived, like the horse, by the Cordilleran valleys, but the Snakes had not developed biological warfare. In another portion of his *Narrative* David Thompson states ''this disease was caught by the Chipaways (the forest Indians) and the Sieux (of the Plains) about the same time, in the year 1780, by attacking some families of the white people, who had it, and wearing their clothes.''

Smallpox was a factor in the final removal of the Kootenay from the plains, decimating their small numbers so severely they never fully recovered. ''They have been in this state ever since the time of the Small Pox in the summer 1781 which swept away nearly whole nations,'' Peter Fidler reports. Four decades earlier the Kootenay suffered another scourge described by the ethnologist Claude E. Schaeffer in his study of the Michel Plains Kootenay:

> The leader of that band at this time was Charcoal Bull. The Kutenai raiders in spring went against the Shoshoni camps. Several warriors entered a lodge and found a dead man inside. Two novices who had been warned not to touch anything in the lodge, removed a pair of decorated moccasins from the body. They did not reveal their action but one donned the footgear at the east end of the Crowsnest Pass. Both he and his friend became ill and the sickness was contracted by the other raiders. Those people of the camp who

could still travel moved eastward through the pass so as not to impart the sickness to Kutenai farther west.

The Kootenay knew the Rockies' geography well. They used the Crowsnest Pass, but they would not camp beneath Turtle Mountain, folklore persists, for they believed the mountain moved. Events bore out their fears on the morning of April 29, 1903, when a chunk of the mountain collapsed and buried much of the coal-mining town of Frank, killing about seventy people. The Kootenay also used the three passes named for them, the North, Middle, and South Kootenay Passes adjacent to Waterton National Park. The Michel Plains People probably used Elk Pass, and the South and North Kananaskis Passes. Archaeological investigations in Yoho National Park reveal a trail that proceeded from the Kootenay River and Valley to the Beaverfoot River, thence to the Kicking Horse River. Alternatively they proceeded by Ochre Creek from the Vermilion River to its summit, descending by the Ottertail River to the Kicking Horse. From the Kicking Horse River the trail proceeded north via the Emerald River, which flows out of Emerald Lake, then crossed over a small summit ridge to the Amiskwi River, up the Amiskwi to Amiskwi Pass, to the Blaeberry River and Howse Pass, which they crossed to the eastward-flowing Howse River, which joins the North Saskatchewan River in Banff National Park. Travelling along the Saskatchewan to the Kootenay Plains was easy. Caches of ochre found in Yoho Park indicate the travellers in that region may have been carrying the material for trade purposes. With routes in the Kananaskis and Elk River regions, Cross Pass and the Cross River, Vermilion and Simpson Passes, the Bow, Cascade, Clearwater, and the Ram River Valleys, the Howse River and the North Saskatchewan, the Kootenay used most transmontane routes in the central and southern Canadian Rockies.

In addition to the movement of the Stoney, one other migration in the shifting mosaic of Indian life in the Rockies was proceeding in the seventeenth century. The language of the Sarcee, a tribe of the Déné, is closely related to that of the Beaver Indians of the woodland north. Their legend is fascinating tale-telling. They were crossing a lake when a child among them saw a monster below the ice. The monster rose up, cracking the ice, and separated the tribe into two bands. Half of them fled north. The others fled south, the Sarcee who now live in the foothills near Calgary. The southern Sarcee had become a plains culture and were already noted equestrians when they came into contact with fur traders. They'd earned a reputation for their hardiness, their dauntlessness in battle, and their bravery, facing, as Alexander Henry the Younger notes, ten times their number without fear. Migrating south, the Sarcee fell under the sway of the Blackfoot Indians, adopting many of their traits and cultural elements. In the eighteenth century they lived and hunted in the North Saskatchewan headwaters region where they developed anew a woodland life. By the early nineteenth century they resided in the Bow River region.

In the eighteenth century the fur trade colonized more and more of the Woodland Peoples of the Saskatchewan drainage. The Seven Years' War, in which England captured the St Lawrence region from France, extended British influence in North America. The American rebellion in the late eighteenth century severed the English market from American fur traders in the Great Lakes region. With Yankee ingenuity, several Americans allied themselves with Montreal traders, creating the North West Company, and, using the Indians' knowledge, developed a route from the St Lawrence drainage by the Lake of the Woods, skirting Hudson's Bay Company territory, crossing it in Manitoba and Saskatchewan, and dropping into the Arctic watershed at the famous Methy Portage in northern Saskatchewan. The route provided access to the Peace-Athabasca delta and its bounty of muskrat many thousand kilometres from Montreal. The development of extended trading routes depended critically on the technology of the Eastern Woodland Indians, the birchbark canoe in particular.

In the late eighteenth century the Hudson's Bay Company established a fort in the foothills on the upper Bow River. The Rockies west of the fort were rich in game but deficient in fur-bearing animals like beaver, otter and muskrat. Why then build a fort there? Two reasons compelled its establishment: trade with the Indians living in the lee of the Rockies, and the hope of a leap across the Rockies into the Pacific watershed. The Plains People, who lived south of the fur-bearing regions, abhorred the fur trade's influence so close to them, and feared one consequence would be the arming of the Cree and the Kootenay who lived near them. The people of the foothills and the mountains already feared the Blackfoot. Intertribal instability in the foothills doomed the fort's fur-trading purpose.

In the late spring of 1793, farther north where the Peace River cuts easterly through the low Rockies, a group of Sekani Indians—literally People of the Rock in their Déné language; that is to say, Rocky Mountain Indians—were disconcerted by a presence they'd heard of but had never seen. Old World trade items had already reached them: some from the fur trade development in the Muskrat Country, some from the Coast Indians' trade with both Russians and English ships which had sailed British Columbia's coastline. The Sekani had never seen white men.

Alexander Mackenzie of the North West Company in 1789 had tried to reach the Pacific Ocean—and ran the river now bearing his name instead. In the autumn of 1792 he set out on a different route, the Peace River—which, uniquely among the rivers of the Rockies, flows through them. That October he proceeded upstream on the Peace River from Fort Chipewyan on "The Lake of the Hills" (Lake Athabasca) to Peace Point, so called because it marked a line of truce between the Cree—whom Mackenzie calls the Knistenaux—and the Beaver Indians they'd displaced. At Fork Fort, nine kilometres upstream from the confluence of the Peace and the Smoky rivers and hundreds of kilometres north and east of the mountains, Mackenzie set up winter quarters. Mackenzie's description places some natives in the region:

> Among the people who were now here, there were two Rocky Mountain Indians, who declared, that the people to whom we had given that denomination, are by no means entitled to it....They said, in support of their assertion, that these people were entirely ignorant of those parts which are adjacent to the mountain[s], as well as the navigation of the river; that the Beaver Indians had greatly encroached upon them, and would soon force them to retire to the foot of those mountains.

All the peoples Mackenzie refers to are Déné, Woodland Indians of the north. The Cree, extending their lands westward with the fur trade to exploit a larger pelt-bearing region, equipped with superior weapons, rifles, and European technology, had but recently displaced the Beaver Indians, who, in turn, moved west toward the northern foothills of the Rockies, displacing the Sekani.

After wintering over, Mackenzie's party in May, 1793, started anew for the Pacific. In five days' travel he, his canoeists, and the Beaver Indians guiding them first glimpsed the Rockies. Another month of hard upriver ascent, which included lining canoes through severe rapids in canyons, brought Mackenzie and his party near the mouth of the Finlay River where they encountered the Sekani, who fled when they first beheld white men. Gradually overcoming their fright, the Sekani finally emerged from the forest to meet the fur traders. They confirmed the existence of trade routes in the forested wilderness of northern British Columbia from the mountain heights to the ocean, for among their possessions was a bone-handled, steel-bladed knife they could have obtained only by trade from the coast.

The Sekani lived in pit houses in winter, in what Mackenzie calls ''sheds'' in summer. They subsisted on small animals and by fishing. Dressed in rough furs and hides, the Sekani manifested the harsh and lonely conditions of their lives in their timorousness.

In the greater part of the Canadian Rockies, the high-peaked, narrow-valleyed ranges most familiar to the visitors of today, the fur trade meant little. Relatively few beaver, otter, muskrat, marten, or foxes lived in the higher mountains. The residents of the fur-impoverished regions had little reason to trap. Thus the fur trade may have depopulated the mountains as the economic persuasion of trapping and trading drew out the Mountain Cree, the Kootenay, the Shuswap, the Sekani, and the Salish who had lived in their shadows for centuries.

3

Strangers in the Land

In the late eighteenth century, about 1798, a group of Iroquois, Algonquin, and Nipissing Indians reached western Canada. Having almost eradicated the beaver in their regions of the St Lawrence and New Brunswick with steel traps, but having learned the ways of the fur trade, they thought they would bring their techniques to the west. The Iroquis did not become dominant in western Canada. Tekarra Peak near Jasper, named by Dr James Hector for an Iroquois who accompanied him in the Athabasca Valley in 1859, is the most substantial reminder of their presence. The superior attitudes of the Iroquois kindled animosity in the plains and foothill dwellers. At the end of one summer the Algonquin and Nipissing headed north for the bushland and its beaver, co-operating with the Parkland Cree "who did not in the least molest them," according to David Thompson. He noted that the Iroquois, contemptuously ignoring the warnings of old hands in the area, headed for the foothills where the beaver were plentiful:

> We pointed out the dangers they would encounter, as it was the country of the powerful tribes of the Plains who had gained the country by war, and held it as a conquered country open to the incursions of their enemies, in which they would probably be destroyed, or at least plundered; by some of the war parties; and advised them to go to the forest lands of the north where there were also many Beaver, the Natives few and peaceable, and where they could hunt in safety....This advice had a very different effect on the Iroquois, who determined to send off a large party to examine the country to the southward and see what the disposition of the Natives were to them, whom they appeared to despise. Accordingly part hunted near the Fort [Augustus] while a party of about seventy five men well armed went off, foolishly taking their self conceit and arrogance with them.

A camp of Peigan, knowing not what to make of the headstrong Iroquois, allowed them to pass, and the easterners proceeded toward the foothills. They passed two more small camps, then after some 135 kilometres of travel, met a larger camp of "Willow Indians." (J. B. Tyrrell, the explorer and historian who edited the first publication of David Thompson's *Narrative*, believes the Willow Indians may have been Shuswaps, "Atsina or Fall Indians, whose country was on the upper waters of the Red Deer River." I surmise the Willow Indians were Stoney, then just reaching the foothills area, the Swampy Ground Stoney referred to elsewhere by Thompson. Another source thinks they may have been Gros Ventre Indians, since displaced to Montana. The Iroquois, speaking little of the local languages, can have defined the tribe only vaguely for Thompson.) The local Indians greeted the strangers hospitably, sharing the pipe with them and feasting. When the strangers invited their hosts to a gambling match, things got out of hand, and Thompson reports "the arrogant gestures of the Iroquois made the other party seize their arms, and with their guns and Arrows lay dead twenty five of them." They retreated rapidly.

The Iroquois, returning to Fort Augustus, invited the Cree to join them in a raid of revenge, but the Cree would have nothing to do with it, warning the Iroquois none of them would survive. The Iroquois decided they'd go back to trapping for the winter. At a farewell feast before they left, the Iroquois performed their "dance of the grand Calumet," then asked the Cree to dance their smoking dance, intimidating the Cree, who had no such dance. Then the exultant Iroquois, "in their best dresses," danced their "War dance, from the discovery of the enemy to the attack and scalping of the dead, and the war hoop of victory." They again challenged the Cree, who had admired the dance, to perform their war dance, "intimating they had none, which was in a manner saying they were not warriors." Pressed to compete by Thompson, "a fine, stern warrior of about fifty years of age," Spikannogan (the Gun Case), stunned the Iroquois to silence by his dance, which the Iroquois thought "war itself to victory and to death." The dance so affected them, "it seemed to bring them to their senses," Thompson says. In days they turned again to trapping, choosing "their hunting grounds to the westward and northward among the forests at the east foot of the Rocky Mountains."

The Blackfoot Nation continued to oppose the North West Company's efforts to cross the Rockies, fearing the trade would arm their enemies to the west in the Rocky Mountain Trench. In July, 1806, Captain Meriwether Lewis of the late-to-reach-the-Rockies Lewis and Clark Expedition murdered two Blackfoot in the Missouri River region. The Blackfoot set out for the south and revenge.

Nineteen years earlier the War Chief of the Peigan, Kootenae Appe (his name means Kootenay Man in Blackfoot) had met the young Thompson in the Bow River region when Thompson was in service with the Hudson's Bay Company. Then, in January, 1788, while Saukamappee had been telling the surveying student how the horse came to the plains and how the Blackfoot had conquered the Bow River country, a "noble specimen of the Indian warrior of the great plains" entered the tent, and presented his left hand to Thompson, who extended his right in return. Saukamappee did not inform Thompson that "the right hand is no mark of friendship," until the party met Indians who had never seen white men before, when he said: "This hand wields the spear, draws the Bow and the trigger of the gun; it is the hand of death. The left hand is next to the heart and speaks truth and friendship, it holds the shield of protection and is the hand of life."

Kootenae Appe graciously ignored the young fur trader's gaucherie. Thompson describes Appe as "six feet six inches, tall and erect, he appeared to be of Bone and Sinew with no more flesh, than absolutely required; his countenance manly, but not stern, his features prominent, nose somewhat aquiline, his manners kind and mild.''

Thompson, now a partner of the North West Company, forced his way across the Rockies in 1807. In August his group constructed Kootenae House on the headwaters of the Columbia River, near what is now Invermere, British Columbia. Appe as War Chief had been leading his warriors south on their mission of revenge against Captain Lewis. The Peigan, furious that the wily Thompson had seized the chance to slip past them, sent a small party to Kootenae House to intimidate him. Any Blackfoot Nation activity in the Rockies was rare; the threat posed by the trade in arms to the Kootenay demanded they overcome their fear of mountains. The Peigan scouts returned to the prairie without intimidating Thompson or the Kootenay Indians with whom he was developing trade. But, Thompson relates, the Peigan—Sakatow the Civil Chief in particular—interpreted his incursion across the Rockies as tantamount to war:

> The Civil Chief harangued them, and gave his advice to form a strong war party under Kootenae Appee the War Chief and directly to crush the white Men and the Natives on the west side of the Mountains, before they became well armed. They have always been our slaves (Prisoners) and now they will pretend to equal us; no, we must not suffer this, we must at once crush them. We know them to be desperate Men, and we must destroy them, before they become too powerful for us.

Kootenae Appe in his turn spoke of how unjust war would be, breaking peace with Thompson and his fur traders, the people with whom they had camped and hunted for ten years. But, Appe declared, if it were the tribe's will, he would lead a troop across the mountains, although without the usual prayers to the Great Spirit for success. Announcing their departure in ten days, he ordered his warriors to prepare.

On the eve of departure, he ordered no shot be fired while the party was travelling ''or we shall be discovered.'' Crossing the mountains, they camped in the valley about thirty kilometres from Thompson's Kootenae House. Thompson welcomed two Peigan, who arrived by another route to ''see the strength of the House.'' They stayed the night. The following morning he asked them how they proposed to recross the mountains. They pointed north. Thompson suggested they take gifts to Kootenae Appe's war camp first, a day thence, intimating he could not assure them any protection from the Kootenay, ''for you know you are on these lands as Enemies.'' Thompson later learned one Peigan chief, upon being presented with the gifts, said:

> You all know me, who I am, and what I am; I have attacked Tents, my knife

> could cut through them, and our enemies had no defence against us, and I am ready to do so again, but to go and fight against Logs of Wood, that a Ball cannot go through, and with people we cannot see and with whom we are at peace, is what I am averse to, I go no further. He then cut the end of the Tobacco, filled the red pipe, fitted the stem, and handed it to Kootanae Appee, saying it was not you that brought us here, but the foolish Sakatow (Civil Chief) who, himself never goes to War.

Then they all smoked, Thompson reports, taking the gift of tobacco with them, and returned across the mountains to the plains, "very much to the satisfaction of...my steady friend [Kootanae Appe]."

In 1808 Thompson returned east across the Rockies with a load of furs, again using Howse Pass and the Saskatchewan River. In late October he returned to the mountains' western side. He had brought the Kootenay Indians into the fur trade in force. In 1809, Thompson started considering an alternative route across the mountains "as at present we are too much exposed to the incursions of the Peegan Indians." By then he had already extended his trading area south into what is now western Montana, developing Saleesh House among the Plateau Indians. In June, 1810, Thompson and his Nor'Westers returned east with a brigade of furs, crossing the mountains guided by a Chipewyan Indian named Pembok. Woodland Peoples, as usual, were aiding the expansion of the fur trade.

That autumn Thompson decided on a new route through the Rockies, one that would provide a necessary detour around the Peigan. Travelling north on a foothills trail on the eastern slope, probably an ancient trail of the Kootenay Indians, with "Thomas an Iroquois Indian as Guide," Thompson and his party abandoned the Saskatchewan watershed for the Athabasca valley. In early November Thomas indicated the party could no longer proceed with horses, and that they should prepare sleds and snowshoes for a winter crossing of a pass he would show them. In twelve years the Iroquois had learned much about the mountain environment, and Thomas led the party safely across the daunting Athabasca Pass in deepest January, the worst time of the year for such a journey.

4

Calling Cards 1840-1870

By 1840 the Mountain Peoples were not moving around as much as they had in the previous half-century. The Mountain Stoney lived in the foothills and the Front Ranges of the Rockies between the Highwood River to the south and the Brazeau River to the north. The Kootenay continued crossing the mountains to hunt bison, but they lived near Columbia Lake in the Rocky Mountain Trench on the western slopes of the Rockies. On the Athabasca headwaters lived some Shuswap, Cree, and the remnant groups of Iroquois whose cultural identity was disappearing generation by generation. Farther north, where the Peace River slices through the mountains, the Western Beaver Indians were happy in their realm; to the west lived the Sekani and the Salish. In the south where the prairie abruptly surges to mountain stronghold, the Blood and Peigan of the Blackfoot Confederacy lived in the immediate lee of the ranges. West of them, along the Kootenay River and in the Tobacco Plains, dwelt more Kootenay and Plateau Indians. Of those people who now call the mountains and their outliers home, only the Sarcee, living under the cape of the Blackfoot, had not become permanent residents.

More changes would affect plains and mountain societies in the next generation than in the previous two. The Plains People would attain their greatest wealth, mobility, and power, then soul-crushingly lose almost everything in the bison annihilation. The Déné and the Mountain People would feel the base of their lives shaken as the fur trade withered; new anxieties would develop as hungry neighbours cast envious eyes upon their domains. Missionaries and a new gospel would come among them, and, from the south, liquor in greater quantity than the fur trade had provided. Trauma would erupt in virtual civil war; a new law and a new order would be imposed from without. The Indian lands would be taken over and the people would be confined on reserves. Smallpox would again run rampant among them; the bison would vanish; starvation would stare from their gaunt faces. Those who had known freedom would become captive nations, rarely to know the wild spirit that illuminated life in the generations receding to the darkness before the dawn of their memory.

The past lived on, surviving in tales the elders remembered, tales that began or ended "This was in the old days." Marius Barbeau, an eminent ethnologist and folklorist, recorded many of the shining legends of the Stoney in the 1920s. I have adapted the Crooked Neck stories and the other Stoney legends and tales from his *Indian Days on the Western Prairie.*

Heroes of nationhood, verified by legends' seal, the giants who walked among them, protecting them, the truth of myth: these facts the Stoney remember in their old testament.

Long ago, when the Blackfoot came to steal horses from the Stoney, Crooked Neck, a great Stoney warrior, changed himself into a mountain lion, falling among them and driving them over a steep river bank in darkness, killing them.

Crooked Neck: mist and magic surround his name, fabulous stories recalling him. In a skirmish, while Crooked Neck and four tribesmen were going to Edmonton, "from way up in the mountains," some Blackfoot shot and killed his mother. Crooked Neck vowed revenge. Crooked Neck's party numbered four; the Blackfoot numbered five thousand. The other men loaded three rifles while Crooked Neck shot. He never tired. Bullets never entered his body. He shot nine hundred Blackfoot. Guns could fire accurately only within a hundred yards. Four days of shooting. Crooked Neck said, "Let us go away! I am tired of killing people. I am sick of shooting." Turning to the battlefield, he started yelling at the Blackfoot who shot back, "but their shots were lost...in the air, just making a noise."

When Crooked Neck met some Blackfoot, bullets flowed from the mouth of one of them. Crooked Neck outdid him. By hitting his hand against his head "a lot of gunpowder exploded....That is the way it happened. There were no people close to him. Every time he hit his head, the powder came out of his mouth and exploded." The frightened Blackfoot ran away.

An old Blackfoot, bragging he used to kill Stoneys near Minnihappa Waterfall, the falls on Cascade Mountain, provoked Crooked Neck's anger. The other warriors had to hold him back. Bear's Paw, the chief, said to Crooked Neck, "Do not fight any more. They fear you anyhow."

Bear's Paw's mother was hunting porcupine. Some Bloods killed her. When she did not return, Bear's Paw sought those who killed her. A Blood, a stranger, came to their camp. Bear's Paw went to him. The Blood extended his hand, greeting him, "Hello, hello, my friend." Bear's Paw aimed his rifle and fired, saying, "That was what I was looking for."

Some Plains People came up the Bow Valley to where the Stoney were camped by Wontshanerawapta, the Ghost River, and in the night stole their horses. Tchakta the Stoney prophet, taking his dream drum and spirit rattle into the medicine lodge, a tepee, sang and invoked a vision of two camps, one of the Blackfoot, one of the Bloods. He foresaw the Bloods killing any party of Stoney braves who might raid their camp. He then chose the braves who would raid the Blackfoot camp for their horses: Wolf Sitting on the View, Big Long Person, Big Hands or Wolf's Ears, Trail Follower, Bear's Paw—a young man then—and Wolf Pillow.

Before dawn the raiding party left the valley of Minisniwapta, the Cold Water River, the Bow River of today. They travelled all day, concealing themselves in the bush. Wind came up, and snow fell in the night. Wolf Sitting on the View, the scout, transformed himself into a wolf and, approaching the Blackfoot camp, travelled silently as a wolf. During the day he spied on some women talking and, listening carefully, learned which horses the Blackfoot considered best. As day drew to a close, he howled like a wolf, and the other Stoney crept through the darkness to meet him.

In the cape of night, Wolf Sitting on the View crept by a dozing Blackfoot guard holding a horse by a rawhide rein. His back to the storm and his horse, the Blackfoot had pulled his blanket over his head for warmth. Wolf cut the tether and silently led the horse away. The Blackfoot never knew.

The other raiders crept toward the camp, Big Hands crawling right into it. Wolf Pillow and Trail Follower, becoming fearful, would go no further. Big Hands gathered five horses, but they were all nags. Near dawn, all the men becoming anxious, Big Hands again crept into the camp and roped ten more horses together. Then the raiders drove their captured horses down to the Minisniwapta. Bear's Paw had separated from the party, so they stopped to decide whether they should go back to rescue him. "If he did not come back after the sun had risen, they meant to go back to the Blackfoot camp." At sunrise, Bear's Paw arrived galloping on a bay horse, leading a black horse.

While the braves had been away, the Stoney camp had moved north toward the Ya-Ha-Tinda, the Meadow in the Mountains. When the braves rejoined their band, all rejoiced in songs of happiness.

In the summer of 1841, Peechee (or Piché), a Métis raised by Cree, a chief of the Mountain Cree who lived by a large lake in the mountains with his family, entered the Rockies by the valley of the upper Ghost River. He was guiding the most powerful man in western Canada, Sir George Simpson, governor of the Hudson's Bay Company. Journeying swiftly, the party proceeded by a peak, Devil's Head, toward the lake where Peechee lived. Simpson in his *Narrative of a Journey Round the World* provides the poignant portrait of his guide and of his mountain home beside the lake now called Minnewanka:

> In the morning we entered a defile between mountainous ridges....This valley, which was from two to three miles in width, contained four beautiful lakes, communicating with each other by small streams; and the fourth of the series, which was about fifteen miles by three, we named after Peechee, as being our guide's usual home. At this place he expected to find his family; but Madame Peechee and the children had left their encampment, probably on account of a scarcity of game. What an idea of the loneliness and precariousness of savage life does this single glimpse of the biographies of the Peechees suggest!

Sir George named the lake Peechee's Lake for his guide; in later years it became first Wendigo Lake, then Lake Minnewanka; in later years surveyors who read Simpson's account, then nearly forgotten, named a mountain nearby for Peechee.

Some years before, the lake and its valley had been the scene of a stirring story Sir George tells. Five youths of a hostile tribe tracked a Cree and his wife from the parkland region into the mountain valley. The man thought they should surrender, but the woman asserted they should defend themselves stoutly since they had but one life to lose: "as they were young and by no means pitiful, they had an additional motive for preventing their hearts from [be]coming small." Taking the rifle for their defence, she dropped "the foremost warrior," and provoked her husband to action with his bow and arrow. He felled two more maurauders. Simpson concludes the tale quickly: "The fourth, who had by this time come to pretty close quarters, was ready to take vengeance on the courageous woman, with uplifted tomahawk, when he stumbled and fell; and in the twinkling of an eye, the dagger of his intended victim was buried in his heart. Dismayed at the death of his four companions, the sole survivor of the assailing party saved himself by flight."

Peechee guided the party by way of the Cascade River to the Bow River, passing the waterfall on Cascade Mountain and, farther west, crossed the Bow River at a traditional ford and ascended by a "road" to the pass that now bears Simpson's name at the summit of Healy Creek. Peechee's party of fur traders was the first group of non-Indians to use the generations-old, rough trail. Several days of difficult travel brought the party to the Columbia River where Simpson met a Kootenay chief whose son he'd taken into his care for education in Fort Garry. The boy, "a fine, clever, docile lad, died—a blow from which the father never recovered." Mentioning the deceased lad, Simpson says, would have breached etiquette severely, but his thoughts and the father's were all on the boy.

Mah-Min, the Stoney chief whom Paul Kane portrayed in a magnificent painting, was among the first of his tribe to become Christian. In 1941, a century after the events, William and Joshua Twin, descendants of Mah-Min's band, told a story of how the Stoney met the Reverend Robert Rundle at Rocky Mountain House. Game was meagre that winter, and the people's hunger was growing. They went to Mah-Min and his brother, and asked them if they could not hear the children crying from their hunger.

The chiefs sang to their gods to find success in a hunt. In the midst of their singing one of the two chiefs suddenly stopped and listened. The people wondered what was happening. He told them a strange voice had spoken to him. Silence fell upon them all. The people asked him to tell them what the voice had said. The voice, he said, told him to stop singing, and to "watch and listen for a white missionary who will come to this country of yours at the time of the next moon." The voice continued: "When the snow is gone and when that missionary comes he will tell you about a Father God in Heaven, and if he tells you about this God, that is very true. You believe in that God and leave me alone for I cannot help you any more.''

The story came true, the Twins continued. The next day hunters shot two moose, and the following day came across a herd of bison and shot many of them, and the people were no longer hungry. ''When it was the time for the dream to come true,...the Stoney Indians made up their minds some of the young men should go to the old fort at Rocky Mountain House—so next day they went and in a few days they came back looking very sad.'' When they set out for the old fort they had gone in full war paint and costume. When they returned their faces were ''clean and washed.'' Those who met Rundle persuaded the others in their band to accompany them on a subsequent journey to meet him. ''The Stoneys were glad they had known a missionary was to come,'' the Twins said, ''and they received him kindly.''

> The missionary began to ring the bell to have a service right on the Stoney Indians' camp ground. The Blackfeet were there too, but they were angry and did not care for the preaching about a father in Heaven. The Stoney Indians believed in God's word. They were very quiet while they worshipped and Rundle preached. Ever since the Stoneys have loved God and loved each other because Rundle told them not to kill anyone.

The Twins added that Rundle never cooked for himself but that the Stoney women cooked for him. In time the missionary told the Stoneys he would have to leave them and return to the east, but promised to come back to see them again some time. ''They felt very lonely for him for he never came back again, for they said, 'We will meet him by and by.' ''

On his way to Rocky Mountain House Rundle translated the words of the hymn ''In the Sweet By and By'' into Cree, the only native language he knew before he met the Stoney. One of their favourite hymns, it is echoed in the Twins' recollections of Rundle. At my grandmother's funeral the Stoney sang it in their own language. Recalling it now, I find it a unique touchstone with the history of the Rockies.

Christianity in the form of Roman Catholicism had already penetrated the forest realm to the north with the fur trade. At a storm's end, observing a rainbow with his Indian companions, David Thompson was pleased to hear their interpretation of the arc as a sign of peace. As we can call no language primitive, neither can we say any religion is simple. Varied sophisticated faiths of the Amerindians prepared them well for Christianity in its divers forms.

Tchakta, the seer who had foreseen the success of the Stoney raiding party against the Blackfoot, also travelled to the Rocky Mountain House region with his family in the early 1840s. When the invitation to baptism came, he came forth rapidly. His conversion was complete, the Stoney recalled for

Marius Barbeau in the 1920s: "He believed in Christianity so strongly that when he heard of war or shooting, he would go into a fast, not eating."

The Stoney who had been, say, Mountain Sheep Woman or Waterfall Girl, Lynx's Eyes or Spotted Eagle, became Leah or Sarah, Benjamin or Joseph: Hebrew and western European first names cropping up in the wake of Robert Rundle, the Wesleyan missionary who baptized and married the Stoney and baptized their children. For seven years he pursued the nomadic peoples of the plains, parkland, foothills, and mountains, never establishing a mission or building, but seeking his flock as it wandered. He was, like his congregation, a child of the sky, the copse his cathedral, and the Stoney found his innocence amenable. Paul Kane attributes part of the fascination Rundle held for the Indians to his pet cat, which he carried on his horse wherever he travelled.

Sir George Simpson had little time for the roving missionary, believing Rundle's translators were inept and his aides bunglers. When the Protestant missionary met the roving Belgian Catholic priest Pierre Jean de Smet on the upper Saskatchewan River, he railed in his journal against de Smet's "popery," but he impressed Père de Smet so little the priest failed to remark upon the event. Rundle's problems may have developed because some Indians believed he was the white man's god. During a service Rundle was delivering to the Blackfoot his translator balked, refusing to go on. Rundle became flustered, and if he had had prospective converts among the Blackfoot, their belief in the new god's infallibility never again rested on so firm a foundation as it had. Yet, despite Rundle's shortcomings, the seeds he sowed bore fruit for future missionaries.

Hector Crawler, a chief of the Wesleys a generation later, was the son of the Stoney seer, Tchakta. (The Wesley Band, one of the three Morley bands, are so called because Robert Rundle, of course, was a Wesleyan missionary.) When he was an old man, Hector Crawler told Marius Barbeau of an earlier Stoney prophet, Face Anything, who foretold the coming of the missionaries. The Stoney of the Rockies, Crawler said, had not seen any white men, and when the first white men to arrive were Hudson's Bay Company traders with liquor in a barrel, they were certain "the spirit of the white men had come." Their medicine man told them they were wrong, those men did not speak for the One who owns all stars, the moon, the sun and all of creation. The preacher arrived—Chief Crawler identified him as a Presbyterian—and told the Stoney to burn all their totems, bear heads, carved figures of animals and birds, saying they were only images, and if they did not burn them as he said they would not enter the land above to meet their departed relatives.

Marius Barbeau reported Hector Crawler's ironic thoughts on the new religion:

> Ever since, the Methodists, Presbyterians, and Catholics have tried to explain to the Prairie Indians about religion. They, the Indians, laughed at them. They said, 'They are trying to get us into a corral. They put us down

as babies. They are trying to tell us the fire water is wrong. How is that—the happiest thing they have brought to us! They try to keep down all the happiness of life. They are greedy; they tell us to have only one wife. And see, some of us have ten wives. They fear the Indians, because they have lots of horses. Big feeling! Everybody is afraid of the chief, because he is big. I think the white people are jealous of him, so they talk like that.'

Chief Crawler himself, about 1914, instigated a revival of the Ghost Dance religion at the Morley Reserve, a radical resurgence of traditional Sioux values that had developed initially in the northern United States.

About 1840 a group of fifteen or twenty Shuswap at Jasper House were startled by a white man they believed—briefly at least—to be "a relation of the Great Spirit." The trader at the fort, a Scots piper, had been in Sir George Simpson's entourage. The Shuswap, hearing the pipes' glorious wail, thought surely such sounds could not emanate from a mortal like themselves. When one Shuswap asked the piper, Colin Fraser, to intercede with the Great Spirit on his behalf, the Highlander remarked he had limited influence in that quarter. The painter Paul Kane, then travelling widely in the west seeking Indian subjects, recorded the incident, adding that the Shuswap had travelled east from their usual home north of the Cariboo Mountains and met a hostile, unnamed tribe, who invited the Shuswap "to sit down and smoke the pipe of peace." Kane's story ends tragically, for the Shuswap "unsuspectingly laid down their arms, but before they had time to smoke, their treacherous hosts seized their arms and murdered them all except eleven, who managed to escape, and fled to Jasper's House, where they remained, never daring to return to their own country through the hostile tribe."

Returning via Jasper House in November a year later, Kane noted two Indians of an unspecified tribe making their way across what he calls Jasper's Lake in a gale:

> The Indians, when they come to ice or hard frozen snow, where the snow shoe has to be taken off, always take off their moccasins also, and travel barefooted; by this means they preserve their moccasins, and when they sit down they put them on dry and wrap their feet in their furs. This walking barefooted on ice in such intense cold would seem dangerous to the inexperienced, but, in fact, the feet of those who are accustomed to it suffer less in this way than they do from the ice which always forms on the inside of the moccasin in long and quick travelling, as the ice thus formed cracks into small pieces and cuts the feet.

The first pictures of western Indians come down to us from the 1840s, for the invasion of the west advanced so rapidly that the prairies and mountains could accommodate artists. The paintings reveal the bison hunters' vigorous lives, ceremonial regalia, pride in station and stature, showing societies at their peaks, presenting subjects in landscapes still part of their traditions. The richly imbued, ornately gladiatorial imagery the paintings sometimes depict reflects European traditions, but they present the regalia accurately, the cultural splendour of the Assiniboines, the Blackfoot, and the Plateau Indians obviously awing the painters.

In 1845 Captain Henry James Warre painted bison hunters in a fanciful light sketch. Near Tsuuptsimtsayankundebi (''If I shoot a little tree mistaken for enemies, I am fooled,'' now known as Canmore), Warre painted the Indians showing his group the way. The expedition, though the Stoney could not have known its mission, presaged the transformation of their world. In the service of the British government, Warre and his companion, Mervin Vavasour, were reconnoitring to see if arms and men could be easily transported across the Rockies to prevent the territory of Oregon from falling into the hands of an expansionist United States. An expansionist British Empire—including Canada—was also looking to its own future.

At Rocky Mountain House in January, 1858, a great Stoney hunter and tracker, whose name translates as ''the one with the thumb like a blunt arrow,'' met a member of another expedition, a group exploring the west's economic potential and locating routes through the Rockies. The young man he met there, James Hector, could not pronounce his Stoney name. Consequently he named him Nimrod. Nimrod promised to guide, hunt and track for him the following summer in the mountains.

In August the Bow River Stoney curiously investigated the new group arriving with carts that it would leave behind when it departed for the higher mountains west. Nimrod, true to his word, showed up as expected. Travelling with the group was the half-Danish linguist Peter Erasmus. A few days later, near the waterfall on Cascade Mountain, the young geologist, Dr James Hector of the Palliser Expedition, whose party it was, met an old Stoney who said he had guided Robert Rundle in the region of the ''little prairie'' near the waterfall Minnehappa and Lake Minnewanka. Nimrod, who had an eye for the beauties of nature as well as the attractions that would appeal to visitors, took Hector to see Bow Falls, upstream from another Stoney campsite.

Though Hector provides eloquent testimony to Nimrod's hunting skills, he relates that near Castle Mountain Nimrod suffered a setback: following an elk, Nimrod shot it, but, pursuing the wounded animal, he ''had fallen on his knife which was stuck in his girdle, and broken it, and one of the pieces had hurt his back severely.'' The injury did not hold him back, for he followed the animal some four miles—''even in summer, when the ground is hard and baked, an Indian can follow their track as easily as we could follow a footpath''—and rejoining Hector, brought him a half-mile to the quarry, ''a fine buck.'' A few days later, reaching Ochre Creek, Nimrod told Hector the Kootenay Indians transformed the ochre with ''a large fire'' into vermilion ''which they take away to trade to the Indians of the low country, and also to the Blackfeet as a pigment.''

The group had difficulty obtaining fresh game, and wet mornings were rotting their preserved moose meat. Famished and worn out, the party turned north on the Kootenay River and reached its headwaters, then descended the Beaverfoot River by an old Kootenay trail to an unnamed wild torrent. There Hector's horse kicked him, providing the name, Kicking Horse, for the stream. For a couple of days Hector recuperated while the party depleted its food. Some evidence indicated Indians, ''probably Shouswaps or Kootanies,'' had been in the neighbourhood in the spring. The party then ascended the Kicking Horse Valley, a perilous journey, and crossed the divide to the Bow River Valley, where Nimrod killed a moose.

In the valley a Stoney family, members of the Wildman family, descendants of Mah-Min, had set up a summer hunting camp. One of the group, ''having smelt our fire a long way off,'' suddenly popped up near Hector's camp, and took the still-injured Hector to the Wildman camp, where the women fed him ''Indian delicacies,—moose nose and entrails, boiled blood and roast kidneys, &c. They had reached this valley, like ourselves, starving, but already there had been killed in the last two days seven moose deer, including Nimrod's one.'' In the camp were two boys, William and Joshua, who took the word twin as their surname. In 1931 William Twin recalled the white men he had met more than seventy years before, the first he had ever seen.

On Sunday the Stoney hymn-singing woke the strangers early, and Hector notes the Stoney did not hunt on Sunday. Three days later, carrying a burden of dried meat the Stoney women had properly prepared, the party departed for the headwaters of the Bow River and the valley of the North Saskatchewan, after tweaking the twins' noses and patting them on their heads. Hector called one mountain to their left on the northward passage Goat Mountain. Today it bears the Stoney name for the white goat, Waputik. A week later Nimrod gave Hector a taste of Stoney lore when Hector invited him to walk on a glacier. ''He would not venture on the ice,'' Hector says, ''but told all sorts of stories of sad disasters that had befallen those Indians that ever did so; how that, if they did not get lost in a crevasse, they were at least sure to be unlucky afterwards in their hunting.''

The Stoney told Hector, when they found some old bison dung, that the animals had been common in the North Saskatchewan Valley a decade before, but disease had broken out among them following a period of great fires, and game was much scarcer than it had been.

Bison were still numerous on the plains to the east of the mountains, but each year, though not noticeably at first, their numbers were decreasing. In 1846 Paul Kane painted scenes of bison hunting in Manitoba. Hunters had so depleted the bison millions in both Canada and the United States by the 1870s that the Plains Indians faced the collapse of their culture in virtual destitution.

Kootenay woman with child in cradleboard, circa 1920. The Kootenay Indians in their transmontane lives spent a portion of their year in typical Plains Indian tepees. The cradleboard shows the richness of Kootenay beadwork, in its geometric symmetry and woodland imagery. Photo by Byron Harmon, courtesy the Whyte Museum of the Canadian Rockies.

5

The Art of Beadwork

On the wall in front of me hangs a blanket strip: three eight-inch beaded circular medallions connected by a wide beaded band. Its utility is decorative. Its Stoney creator made it to sew to a horse blanket for adorning a horse in ceremonial parades; years ago she might have sewn it to a blanket for a man or, less frequently, a woman to wear.

Symmetry describes the design of the piece. Each medallion reflects itself on two axes, as do the bands connecting the medallions. A powder blue field supports small triangular wedges of orange and red. Hourglass shapes, ''arrowheads'' connected at their points, describe the motifs of the bands. It's fine contemporary work.

About four years after she made it, I asked the artist, Reba Bearspaw, a member of the Bearspaw Band of the Stoney, to tell me what the symbols of her work meant. I thought, because she'd created the object recently, she could illuminate its meanings. Intelligent and articulate, like many other artists she preferred to be vague about its meanings. Her very vagueness led me to speculate on the art of beadwork.

Two streams define the beadwork of the Woodland and Plains Peoples, two great streams that flow together in Stoney culture. In one stream flows the floral richness of woodland design: gaily stylized blossoms in patterns as rich as Oriental carpets, the entire surface compulsively filled in. The colours are close to natural: leaves green, blossoms red and yellow and blue. In the other stream flows a geometric ordering of plains motifs and designs: triangles, stepped squares, simple grounds of solid colour, balance and order dominating.

Western Indian peoples, before the fur trade introduced European beads, created their art in quillwork, porcupine quills dyed with vegetable colours, sewn with their own points to a surface of buckskin. The quills were flattened, and could be laid into designs like appliqué, or braided, plaited, or otherwise bent. The quill colours can be bright, but they reflect their vegetable origin, the tones of the Earth and its plants and berries in mauves and purples, engorged reds and lichen-pale yellows. Rare, exquisite, and refined, quillwork to the end of the nineteenth century reflects the same differences as beadwork, imagery derived from nature in the woodland material, geometric imagery in plains traditions. Beads, brighter and easier to work with, replaced the more fragile quills quickly when they became available. Quill length determined the size of pattern shapes.

But I wish to speak not of the crafts of quillwork and beadwork, superb as they may be, but of the art and meanings of Indian design.

Some knowledgeable people argue that French nuns introduced ornate floral designs to the Woodland Peoples of eastern Canada in embroidery patterns. The progress of floral designs in beadwork, they suggest, follows the western march of the fur trade into the woodland interior of Canada, thence into the foothill frontier and mountainous country of both Canada and the United States, even to the Déné-speaking Navajo of the American southwest. The Plains People prized the elaborately adorned quill- or bead-decorated caribou hide jackets—pieced and stitched in the pattern of European clothes of the seventeenth and eighteenth centuries. Woodland People around Hudson Bay made such morning coats and traded them advantageously to the Plains People who admired the pattern, construction, and the craftsmanship of the jackets, but the design elements never became part of their own design vocabulary. Why not? The answer, I believe, lies in the distinct world views of the different peoples. Admiring the works of other cultures, we do not imitate their art unless it satisfies something within us, answering our questions about who we are, our way of life, or why we live where we live.

Woodland religions, I surmise, saw many spirits in the elaborated complexity and texture of their landscape. One creator, perhaps, in many manifestations. Henry Kelsey in 1690 noted that his guides and protectors refused to eat flesh of the grizzly bear, for to them the bear was a god.

> They believe in the self existence of the Keeche Keeche Manito (The Great, Great Spirit)...they appear to derive their belief from tradition, and [believe] that the visible world, with all it's inhabitants, must have been made by some powerful being....he is the master of life, and all things are at his disposal; he is always kind to the human race, and hates to see the blood of mankind on the ground, and sends heavy rain to wash it away. He leaves the human race to their own conduct, but has placed all other living creatures under the care of Manitos (or inferior Angels) all of whom are responsible to him;...each Manito has a separate command and care, as one has the Bison, another the Deer; and thus the whole animal creation is divided amongst them.

The tangled garden of woodland floral design answers to the complex, divers, concealing and revealing pattern of the world in which the Woodland People lived. Floral patterns answered to the world they lived in; hence Woodland People accepted European floral motifs, and embellished them in making them into their art. Spring is the calendar's most important event for northern peoples, the awakening, blossoming universe asserting regeneration and the continuity of life, the defeat of winter once again. Woodland People value most the colours of spring. Prairie People admired the craftsmanship in the complex designs, but the meanings—yea-saying the world in a pantheistic perception of nature's elaborate scrolls there for the reading—did not fulfil their view of the cosmos.

Horizon defines the unity of the universe in the reduced, direct, straightforward plains, world as land and sky. Nothing interrupts the continuity, as forest or mountains do. The mind abstracts perceptions. Land and sky balance physical and chimaerical polarities. If the universe reveal unity in its creation, one creator manifested it. Monotheism, the principle of one god, one creator, expresses the creation of a coherent, perceivable spirit. In their art the Plains People affirm oneness in their balanced, geometric, symmetrical language of forms.

Two streams flow together in Stoney art, as in the art of the Kootenay. Some of it, like Reba Bearspaw's blanket strip, affirms the Plains People's view of the world as a single god's creation, a cosmology of one mind, one world, one creator. Its symbolism is the symbolism of the *mandala,* the circle in the square or the square in the circle, expressing what Carl Jung calls the deepest interpretation of the soul, the stability of the four-sided, four-pointed world—the points to which the Plains Indian directs his pipe—and the unity of the circle. If I am imposing an interpretation on a work Reba Bearspaw could not explain, so be it; its meanings verge on the most arcane symbolism. Many artists, Indian and non-Indian, stumble in their explanation of such symbols. Reba Bearspaw's traditions are rooted in a plains background, if four or more generations removed from experience of it.

Geometry exemplifies the bead art of some other Sioux Nation tribes. One explanation for abstract designs: among some societies men refused women the right to create art representing real objects, since men—medicine men and shamans—retained exclusively the imitation of animistic spirits in their art and theology, obtaining control over animals or plants by their representations of them. Compelled by their imaginations to create art, the women artists resorted to geometry. Anthropologists seeking explanations of beadwork patterns found admirable confusion, the men saying the patterns on their clothing had one set of meanings, the women whose work it was ascribing other meanings to them. Hence my quest to find a deeper rationale for symbolism so common in Stoney bead art.

The beadwork of the Kootenay reflects both woodland and plains motifs: representational symbols like horses, reflecting the long involvement of the Kootenay with the animal; plants and flowers; stylized mountains vying with curves, squares and geometric representation. Often enough the work may reveal the animated psyche of the world in its pictorial content, but the border or frame around the pictorial aspect will be boldly geometric. Pinks and purples are much more common in Kootenay work than they are in the beadwork of the other peoples of the mountains. Colour patterns, motifs, and symbolism seem to have run up and down the Kootenay and Columbia Rivers among the Plateau Indians. Their beadwork, as we should expect, reflects the diversity of all the tribes they came into contact with, as well as the complicated aspects of their lives as horsemen, fishermen, and agriculturally-based peoples, and the divers environments in which they live: the mountains, the river environs, and the arid Tobacco Plains.

The few examples of Sarcee beadwork I have seen and studied reflect again both the transmission of various cultural symbols, the Blackfoot geometries, their own boreal background, and the melding of different traditions. Like Stoney beadwork of the classical period (1880-1920), Sarcee bead art frequently uses the pale blue ground upon which the Stoney place their geometric figures. Sarcee pieces, however, employ woodland motifs of stylized blossoms, some of them so stylized as to seem geometric configurations of the idea of blossoms. (As a cloverleaf is a quadrifolium to a geometer, some Sarcee blossoms seem to derive from a world of mathematical curves.)

Native American costume of the western plains is one of the world's great cultural flowerings. Of buckskin leather rendered soft and supple by brain-tanning, rich in woodsmoke odours, earthy in its tonal range of fawn, brown, and creamy white, the clothes—jackets, dresses, leggings, gloves, and moccasins—provide a tough yet resilient surface on which the artists can invoke their decoration. Fringes of stitched-on buckskin provide epaulettes and frogs, and grace the wearers' motions as they amplify their gestures. The clothing itself integrates the land and its nature. It was a practical clothing: it allowed easy movement; it inhibited the harsh wind; it repelled the barbs of willow, poplar, and grass. Yet it allowed much surface for individual expression, and it endured, neither wearing out easily nor letting fashion pass it by. Handsome and graceful, it wore like a tougher, outer skin. Only in rainy weather did buckskin clothing fail, for then it became sodden, heavy, and cold. But then they could stride most proudly in their robes of fur.

The individuality and the personality of the wearer seemed implicit in each person's costume. Talismans of spirit, fetishes of place, totems of family: the language of costume the Mountain Peoples developed is but whispered, its broad strokes apparent, but its nuances beyond the threshold of a world removed from its original wearer's experience.

6

Capital in Reserve

In good time, in the dusk of the evening, we came in sight of the camp, a veritable moving village, the home of the most nomadic of all peoples in America. To my eye there could be very little more fitting of its kind than an Indian camp, nestling among the valleys, with a background of beautiful foothills, and these, in turn, buttressed by lofty ranges of majestic and imperial mountains. Here the child of nature was at home in nature's lap.

In April, 1873, John McDougall, a Methodist missionary raised in western Canada by his missionary father, George Millward McDougall, visited the Munuchaban (''the place one takes bows from'' in Cree) to see whether the church should establish a mission to the Stoney. In the last of his four volumes of autobiography, *On Western Trails in the Early Seventies,* McDougall recreates his observations of the Mountain Stoney on the brink of catastrophic changes to their lives:

> The offspring of this wild, unfettered life of many centuries, held up thus on his mother's breasts, turned one's thoughts to the future and to these magnificent foothill and mountain breasts, surcharged and bursting with the rich and richer milk of incomputable wealth for the generations yet unborn. The present owners of this great domain were thoughtlessly, carelessly, living on the surface. Like the butterfly flitting from plant to plant, so these men roamed and camped and dreamed not of mines and means which were above and beneath them on every hand. They had never thought of nor speculated upon the magnificent array of mighty power within their sight and sound, and in the centre of which they were living all the time. They worried not because of stacks or stooks, nor yet 'stocks.' They lost neither appetite nor sleep because of marts or merchants. They heard not the clank and clink of multiple machinery, and much less the roar and rush of transcontinentals. None of these thing moved them, for truly it had not entered into their life, nor come as yet into their thought. Sufficient for them was the fact that the sun shone, the waters ran, the dew and rain fell, and mother earth responded gloriously with forest and grass and shrub and fruit. Here the buffalo grazed and grew fat; among these woods the moose and elk browsed and took on in season most exquisite meat; all species of deer and all fur-bearing animals lived and thrived; the creeks and rivers and lakes moved with fish; the seasons followed the one the other in regal succession; life, full and natural, was all around them and above and beneath. So they were amply satisfied.

Within a decade the bison would be extinct, smallpox would sweep from the plains into the valleys of the Rockies again, the chiefs of southern Alberta's tribes would gather at Blackfoot Crossing to sign Treaty #7, the new government would establish reserves, and railway surveyors would foreshadow the construction of the Canadian Pacific Railway.

William Twin, a lad when he had first met white men near Kicking Horse Pass in the 1850s and now almost thirty years old, was in the camp at the Munuchaban in September, 1873, when John McDougall and his brother David—who would become the first merchant in the region—returned. The missionary had travelled to Winnipeg in the summer and had obtained approval for a mission to the Stoney. That September he scouted a site for the mission near the principal ford of the Bow River in the region, near the confluence of the Bow and Ghost Rivers, where a lone Stoney family, the Wildmans, met him. The McDougalls, bound for the upper Highwood River and farther south and needing a guide, hired William. The McDougalls could obtain their supplies more easily in the "Land of the Long Knives"—Montana, where the Americans had established a base for the whiskey trade north across the "Medicine Line," the Forty-Ninth Parallel.

When the party met two Blackfoot in the foothills at the forks of Sheep Creek, Twin demonstrated his linguistic skills, translating their language into the Cree that McDougall spoke. The Blackfoot were snaring eagles to obtain feathers to adorn their war dresses, "the tail feathers especially commanding a high price among these people," McDougall comments. Describing their technique, he says they "caught the eagles by making pits, in which the hunter secreted himself, and his associate covered the mouth of the pit with sticks and grass, and laid pieces of fresh meat thereon; the eagle, alighting to gorge himself, was quietly seized from beneath, and being pulled down, was strangled."

In late November, John, as the Stoney called McDougall, returned north to the Bow Valley where he met the Stoney chief, Bear's Paw, searching for one of his people, Enoch. Some Blood Indians who'd heard Enoch's gunfire while he was hunting had fallen upon him and murdered him. Within two weeks of returning from Montana, aided by James Dickson, his interpreter and aide, whom Robert Rundle had baptized a generation earlier, McDougall, afraid the Plains Indians might come raiding, built a small fort in the timber five kilometres north of the Bow Valley.

A member of Bear's Paw's band, He Who Follows on the Trail, living up to his name, became separated from the body of the band, and a few Blackfoot stole his two ponies. "He set out to interview the Blackfeet," McDougall relates, and "this he did to the tune of twelve horses." Bear's Paw, wondering how a man with two horses came by twelve, let He Who Follows on the Trail keep two of them, but sent the other ten back to the Blackfoot. McDougall praised the act: "Here was evidence of Christian teaching, and even the Blackfoot wondered at such conduct on the part of these Indians who had been their lifelong enemies."

Ambivalent in his respect and admiration for his parish, McDougall reveals his romantic awe for his Stoney flock:

> Here were men familiar with the strong, energetic and constantly exciting and stimulating side of life. The mountains, with snow-slides, and mud-slides, and rock-slides, and sudden avalanches, were their birthplace and hunting grounds. Impetuous, tumbling, rushing, raging mountain streams were their swimming schools. Grizzlies and mountain lions and wildcats were their constant game. Blackfeet, Bloods, Piegans, Sarcees, and often Crees, were their perennial enemies. To run down moose and elk and lynx on foot was their common sport. To climb and carry and starve and feast were their frequent experiences. Among nomads these people excelled; from the head waters of the Missouri to those of the Athabasca, from the Columbia to the heart of the great plains, these people roamed and hunted and fought and conquered. They were a terror to the plains tribes. Before the new evangel reached them, they were inveterate gamblers, and often killed the people of their own tribe in these mad scenes of intense excitement. Such were our new parishioners, and we felt that we needed a large measure of tact and patience to manage and keep the peace with these wild, nervous tribes.

At Christmas McDougall journeyed to Edmonton, returning with his brother David and their wives. John, about that time, named his mission Morleyville for the Reverend Morley Punshon, the Methodist preacher who had endorsed its establishment. Shortened to Morley, it remains the name of the Stoney Indian Reserve and the village midway between Banff and Calgary.

Political currents were swirling about all the peoples of the west. Canada had become a political entity in 1867 and immediately set its sights on expanding westward towards the British colony on the Pacific coast to the west of the mountains. In 1870 the Hudson's Bay Company sold to the fledgling Canada all the lands it held licence to, including the Saskatchewan and Athabasca drainages. In the United States the Union Pacific Railway, completed in 1869, severed the bison herds in twain. The Long Knives of Montana—so called for the length of their swords—were bringing whiskey into the country, and the Plains Indians with the higher-powered firearms they'd obtained from the Americans were slaughtering bison for robes to trade for firewater. Wolvers, hunters, and traders were further decimating and dividing the Canadian herds, one of them still living on the edges of the mountains, foothills, and the parkland frontier, the other centred on the Assiniboine River to the east. In the northern and western United States wars against Indians were raging, and several tribes, like Chief Sitting Bull's Sioux and Chief Joseph's Nez Percé, sought refuge north of the border. The Métis of Manitoba, led by the astute and visionary Louis Riel, foreseeing the rending of the web of their lives, rebelled; and Ottawa, reacting swiftly and sternly, but with perhaps greater humanity than the Americans, created the police force that marched into the west and the lives of the Plains and Mountain Peoples in 1874.

The intertribal wars ended along with most of the raiding, the horse-capturing, the swift retaliations. The flow of liquor from Montana dried up in the presence of the North West Mounted Police. In 1871 British Columbia, beyond the Rockies, became part of Canada, and Canada promised to build a railway to the Pacific coast to seal the bargain. Before the railway had extended beyond Winnipeg, ranchers were driving herds of cattle north from the Missouri Basin into the foothills of the Rockies. John McDougall built a new settlement at Morley closer to the Bow River, out of the woods where he had first established his small wilderness fortress, and his gracious small church on the crest of a hill became a landmark of the Bow Valley.

In the summer of 1877 the moccasin telegraph carried word that all Indians south of the Red Deer River were to gather at Blackfoot Crossing to make treaty. The three Stoney bands—the Bearspaws, the Chinikis, and the Goodstoneys, or the Wesleys as they came to call themselves—heard of the gathering at Blackfoot Crossing on the Bow River in the heart of the Blackfoot Nation's prairie lands, and their chiefs led the Mountain People to meet Queen Victoria's representatives. Bear's Paw and his band were on the Highwood River when they heard the word, and it took many days to assemble and make the journey. From the north, near the headwaters of the North Saskatchewan River, the Goodstoney band began its trek overland to the Bow. The Chinikis proceeded directly from their lodges close by the McDougall Mission. John McDougall attended the great meeting in August, 1877, to interpret for the Stoney.

The Lieutenant-Governor of the North-West Territories, David Laird, spoke as the Queen's representative to the assembled nations:

> ...now the Queen has sent Col. Macleod and myself to ask you to make a treaty. But in a very few years the buffalo will probably all be destroyed, and for this reason the Queen wishes to help you to live in the future in some other way. She wishes you to allow her white children to come and live on your land and raise cattle, and should you agree to this she will assist you to raise cattle and grain, and thus give you the means of living when the buffalo are no more. She will also pay you and your children money every year, which you can spend as you please. By being paid in money you cannot be cheated, as with it you can buy what you may think proper.

The Lieutenant-Governor outlined the specific grants of the treaty: twelve dollars for every man, woman, and child; five dollars for each person every year thereafter; a suit of clothes, a silver medal, a flag, and a larger sum for every chief upon the signing of the treaty, a new "treaty suit" every three years thereafter; and a reserve "upon which none other will be permitted to encroach; for every five persons one square mile will be allotted on this reserve, on which they can cut the trees and brush for firewood and other purposes."

Thus did it come to pass that the Stoney, with the other nations, did "cede, release, surrender, and yield up to the Government of Canada for Her Majesty the Queen and her successors forever, all their rights, titles and privileges whatsoever" to their lands, and the Treaty declared "the reserve of the Stony band of Indians shall be in the vicinity of Morleyville." John McDougall had successfully argued with the authorities on behalf of his parish and parishioners that the Stoney Reserve should lie adjacent to his mission, and so it came to be. Mas-gwa-ah-sid (Bear's Paw) signed for his band; Che-ne-ka (or John) signed for his Chiniki Band; Ki-chi-pot (Jacob Goodstoney) signed for the Wesleys. The missionary had been trying, with marginal success, to train his nomad congregation to become farmers, so the Stoney accepted farming implements rather than the cattle the government gave the Plains People.

The Sarcee, the wandering tribe of Déné, also signed Treaty #7, Stamistocar (Bull Head) holding his hand to the pen that marked his X. The Sarcee Reserve was initially included in the general description for the Blackfoot Reserve on the prairie by the Bow River east of Calgary, but by 1881 Bull Head had expressed eloquently and frequently his disdain for sharing a reserve with the Blackfoot, and he requested a reserve in the foothill country west of Calgary, near the ranches white settlers were then developing. Ottawa feared the Sarcee and the ranchers would develop conflicts, but in June, 1883, the government negotiated a new treaty with the Sarcee, establishing a reserve in perpetuity at the site Bull Head had chosen. By a long journey the Sarcee returned to a wooded area similar to the one they had departed generations before.

In 1881 the first railroad surveyors arrived in the mountains along the Bow River, locating a route for the Canadian Pacific Railway. Near where the Wildman family had aided Dr Hector's party twenty-three years before, Edwin Hunter, a Stoney, met an enthusiastic young man working with the survey party, and in 1882 showed him the way to Ho-run-num-nay, the Lake of the Little Fishes, Lake Louise. Informal as the event was, it held many implications for the tourist trade in the mountains. Tom Wilson, the scout, never claimed he'd discovered the lake which would become a gem in the crown of mountains the railway would promote to visitors. He would, however, become a guide himself, an outfitter, an employer of the Stoney in his business, and in 1889 would instigate Banff Indian Days. The Mountain People he met were still pursuing their ancient ways in the Rockies, hunting and trapping the valleys on both sides of the Great Divide.

A Wesley Band Stoney peers through Elliott Barnes's camera, Kootenay Plains, circa 1907.
Photo by Reginald Holmes, courtesy the Whyte Museum of the Canadian Rockies.

7

Civilization: its Discontents

> Long long ago they tell of there being just two kinds of Indians, the men and the women, and they didn't know of the existence of each other. One time the men were preparing a Buffalo Dead Fall and noticed another tribe of people who looked like themselves and were camped below, so they sent their chief...to investigate, and he brought back the chief of the other tribe. They were the same sort of people, only somehow different, for one tribe was all men, the other all women, and so they decided to stay together, the two tribes, and that is the way their Adam and Eve story started.

George McLean, or Walking Buffalo, the Stoneys' Medicine Man for the period from 1900 to his death on Boxing Day, 1967, was a well-schooled man who also had a lively interest in his tribe's traditions. (The Methodist missionary John Maclean had adopted the lad and named him George Maclean. George used McLean, and his family spells the name that way.) In the 1940s and '50s, George often visited my aunt and uncle, Peter and Catharine Whyte, in Banff. Pete asked the questions; George answered them in his deliberate, articulate fashion; and Catharine made notes of what he said. Pete had asked George where the Stoneys came from and George told him what he called the Stoneys' Adam and Eve story. The tale included a detailed description of the Buffalo Dead Fall:

> Long ago, before the Indians had guns or even bows and arrows, they used to kill the buffalo by running the herd over a cliff and then getting those killed by the fall. This was called the Buffalo Dead Fall. The Indians prepared for this very carefully. They first picked a likely place, and at the foot of the cliff built a strong corral or stockade to hold the animals after they fell. Above, they built a sort of fence...which led the buffalo over the cliff in the right spot, really two fences converging. Beyond that, on the prairie, they stationed every little way an Indian who sat motionless. Then a group of Indians would find a herd of buffalo which they would start moving toward the cliff. As they got nearer, if the herd started moving in the wrong direction, a slight move by one of the motionless Indians would be enough to head them off, and finally they would approach the cliff edge, and before the front ones could stop, the others had pushed them over, for there were thousands of buffalo in a herd. A good many would get away, but there were enough piled up at the foot of the cliff in the corral for the Indians: the buffalo who fell on top of the first to fall over would scramble out and away.

In the ninth decade of the nineteenth century the Paleo-Indians' Old Bow Valley Trail became the Canadian Pacific Railway's route. Surveyors arrived, then construction crews, followed by what George McLean—who was thirteen when the line reached Morley—called fire-wagons, the diamond-stacked, smoke-belching dragons of the railroad. At Morley the line crossed the Stoney reserve on its ascent to the height of the Rockies. (In return for the railway's alienation of their land, the Stoney received a privilege with which they would later harass the railway: any Stoney could flag any train to board for a ride east or west. In the late 1960s when a train killed a horse on the reserve, the CPR's lawyers argued the horse was trespassing, hence the company owed its owner no compensation. When the Stoney's lawyer discovered the unrescinded agreement, the CPR backed down quickly.)

Canada's first National Park emerged at Banff in the wake of the railroad in 1885, and tourists, a Victorian phenomenon, arrived on the first scheduled passenger trains. Because they knew the land and its secrets, some Stoney became guides to the new trade, or supplied horses for adventurers and outfitters. But most of them tried to sustain domestic lives, learning to be farmers or ranchers—not easy for a society nomadic for centuries—or continuing to be trappers and hunters.

Ne-sho-dao (his Stoney name means "embers") or William Twin, born to the Wildman family of the Chiniki Band (also known as the Chiniquay or Che-ne-ka Band) about 1845, became the exemplar of the Stoney as mountain guide. Of all his tribe, Twin most capably adapted to new possibilities. Regretfully, few others of the tribe maintained mountain lives as fully as did William Twin. In 1893 an adventure-seeking group of Philadelphians hired him to bring saddle ponies from Morley to Laggan so they could ride in comfort the few kilometres from the station to Lake Louise's legendary shore. "Horses were so scarce at that time," said Mary Schäffer, a member of the party who wrote an account of the trip, "that Tom Wilson had to send to Morley on the Indian Reserve and 40 miles from Banff to get the horses to take us up to Louise." Tom Wilson, who eleven years before had learned of the lake from Edwin Hunter, had established himself as a guide and outfitter in Banff. The visitors sat atop a boxcar for the trip from Banff to Laggan, "growing blacker and blacker." At their journey's end they met William Twin and his family.

> There were the Indians and their horses as Tom had told us they would be. They had brought their squaws and all their children. To an eastern eye I never saw such a bunch of disappointing horse flesh....
>
> To me the squaws, papooses, and tepees were wonderful and most picturesque but also I was most desirous to get out of that medley of horses the very best one to carry me up some unknown precipitous trail. I went on the basis that an Indian must be very like his white brother and having had to scurry round for myself before, I approached one of the Indians with a half dollar, perfectly within his vision and mine but to no one else. To my disgust

he led me to one of the most forlorn horses in the group, confidentially whispering: 'Him good squaw horse, very good,'' I felt I had wasted a perfectly good coin not to mention I had been selfish into the bargain. But 'William Twin' I soon found had played fair. While all the other horses were wandering all over the trail, taking every advantage of a bunch of easterners who had no idea on earth how to make them go, my wooly, skinny 'Joshua' marched steadily ahead.

The road to Louise at that time was only a semblance of a road. We must have been a funny sight to Mr. Wilson and I believe the distance over that old road was only about 2 miles. Think of those Indians coming over 80 miles of trail to take such an insignificant few up two miles of very nice hill. I felt perfectly delighted with my mount, he had been all a gentleman could be.

No sooner had Mary Schäffer and her friends reached the lake when their itinerary obliged their riding to the Lakes in the Clouds:

I walked naturally over to Joshua to whom I had already become devoted, only to find another member of our party struggling to mount him. Surprised, I said: 'O, that's your horse over there, this is mine.' 'O no. I have had all I want of mine. You have had the best horse this far.'...But dear old William Twin had not forgotten the piece of silver which had changed hands. He had an eye on all our motley crowd and seeing me get the worst of the bargain, I must say I was scared stiff myself when I saw him shake his fist in the little lady's face and order [her] to the horse which had been originally allotted her. It's the only time in all these years I have seen William's face anything but placid and we never meet without both of us talking at once, he in Stoney and I in English. And what is more we both know from our expressions what the other is aiming at. I love the Indians. Do them a good turn and they do not forget. I kept Joshua and he being such a fine trailer, we led the way to the lovely 'lakes of the clouds.'

The next summer, 1894, William Twin met Samuel E.S. Allen of Philadelphia, the son of one of Mary Schäffer's companions, and Walter D. Wilcox, his fellow student at Yale University, and several of their friends who had come to the Rockies for a summer of mapping, exploration, and adventure. Wilcox writes that William Twin "came nearer to a realization of the ideal Indian features such as one sees on coins, or in allegorical figures, than almost any savage I have ever seen." William Twin and Tom Chiniquay both worked for the CPR's chalet at Lake Louise, constructing trails and handymanning for the tiny resort. Wilcox notes the Indians' exceptional eyesight in a telling anecdote. Twin observed a goat herd on a slope and tried to tell the lads where he'd spotted it. A pair of strong binoculars helped the visitors find the "small white spots without definite forms, whereas to the Indians they were plainly visible. William was disgusted with us, and said, 'White man no good eyes,' in evident scorn."

William Twin's education of Samuel Allen resulted in most placenames in the Rockies that have a Stoney origin. Allen, the finest linguist of the young American visitors, earnestly sought from Twin and from other Stoneys working in the area the words he thought would aptly fit the features of the landscape he was exploring and mapping. Minewakun, meaning cascade or small torrent, he placed on a small lake fed by a surging little stream. Wastach, or beautiful, he applied to a pass he crossed that leads to Paradise Valley (a valley he called Wastach). The great peak at the valley's head he named Hungabee, Stoney for chief. The most euphonious name he graced the landscape with, Minnestimma (sleeping water), adorns two small tarns above Larch Valley. The ten peaks of the valley he named for the Stoney numerals from one to ten: Heejee, Nom, Yamnee, Tonsa, Sapta, Shappee, Sagowa, Saknowa, Neptuak, and Wenkchemna. (Seven of the Ten Peaks—the exceptions are Sapta, Neptuak, and Wenkchemna—have been renamed since Allen's day, sometimes reasonably, sometimes ineffectually.) A sharp peak on the Lake O'Hara side he named Yukness, and a rocky pass Opabin, and he named a peak above a place he had called the Gorge of the Winds Wiwaxy or windy.

Sentimentalists occasionally wonder why more Rocky Mountain peaks, rivers, and valleys do not bear Indian names. Samuel Allen established the practice, but few others followed his trailblazing. Wapta, for river, shows up in the paradoxical Wapta Lake, and on the Washmawapta Icefield in the region of the Ice River. To the west of the Bow River headwaters is the Waputik Range, Dr Hector's name, derived from the white goats that live there. John McDougall's biography quotes his aversion to new names: "I protest against the changing of the names by the various geographical factions in the country, from those given by the original inhabitants, as these names as a rule have special significance." McDougall, however, had renamed the Munuchaban, the Place One Takes Bows From, Morleyville. To the point, however, determining Kootenay names for Rockies topography generations after the Kootenay ceased hunting their traditional grounds would be difficult, and Stoney names, except for those Allen so appropriately used, have been rarely recorded.

In one foray in 1894 three members of the Allen-Wilcox group attempted climbing a couloir on Mount Lefroy. A dislodged boulder smashed the leg of one of them. While the injured man awaited rescue, Wilcox raced back to the Lake Louise chalet, only to discover William Twin and Tom Chiniquay were on another slope cutting a trail with the hotel manager. Four hours after the accident occurred the rescue party reached the injured man. Wilcox remarks, "William Twin observed his woebegone appearance and heard his groans with concern, but with true Indian lack of tact, frequently during the painful journey entertained the invalid as follows: 'You think you die? Me think so too.' '' Wilcox, aware of the Stoney aversion to icefields, praised both men for crossing snow bridges ''with perfect coolness, even after one gave way and Chiniky only saved himself by holding on to the pole of the litter.''

Wilcox recounts one personal, revealing aspect of Twin's life. The year before, William had lost his wife and four children to smallpox, still a scourge to these people who had no antibodies to ward off foreign diseases:

> ...it had affected him so that he could not sleep. In his own simple form of expression, it was most pathetic to hear him speak of this sad event, which evidently affected him deeply. 'Me sleep no more now,' he would say, 'all time think me, squaw die, four papoose die, no sleep me. One little boy, me —love little boy, me—little boy die, no longer want to live me.'

In 1895 the first New York Sportsman's show was held in Madison Square Garden. The Canadian Pacific Railway, wishing to exhibit in the show, asked John McDougall to recommend a real ''Grizzly Bear Hunter.'' The preacher chose William Twin, who had already shown himself capable of getting along with tourists, and who could speak English well enough to be part of the CPR's exhibit. McDougall, travelling to Winnipeg himself, accompanied Twin as far as Winnipeg. McDougall's account of the trip is included in the biography *McDougall of Alberta* by John Maclean, himself a Methodist missionary and author:

> I took a section in the sleeper and told William to climb into the upper berth. He had climbed to giddy heights far above the clouds; he had watched the flashes of lightning, and felt the vibrations of thunder shocks below him; he had made his way on craggy ledges, with overhanging rocks above and sombre depths beneath; he had climbed and clung on mountain slopes; he had killed Big Horn Sheep and Mountain Goats, and huge grizzly bears, and now at fifty years of age he was having a new experience. An upper berth in a palatial sleeper, with spotless sheets and downy pillows, was such a radical change that William could not sleep, so with the first peep of day he quietly whispered down to me: 'Are you awake? It is not time to get up?' I replied, 'Turn over and have another snooze.' 'Where are we now?' he whispered. Great was his surprise when I told him we were one hundred and fifty miles from home! When we went to the diner and were seated, William was taking note of everything, and this man, who had spent all his life roaming in the mountains, said to me: 'Now I am in an unknown land, but you know where we are going, and I have faith in you!'

In Winnipeg Twin beheld the small city's cosmopolitan crowd, "the Main Street, the City Hall, the Hotel and the Elevator" awed the "Grizzly Bear Hunter." Evening service at Grace Church with the organ, choirs, galleries, and electric lights similarly filled William with wonder: "What I have seen and heard to-night is greater than all my dreams," he said, and he vowed to "dwell on larger and more beautiful things." In a day Twin and McDougall departed, the Stoney bound for Manhattan, the minister for the Manitoba north.

Philip Moore of Banff, a guide and lecturer on Indian topics, years later asked Twin for his thoughts of New York. "Many canyons of buildings," Twin said. "Walk many miles, find no stream, find no lake, find no poles for lodge. Not very good place for camp." (Determining how formally Twin spoke English is difficult. F. O. "Pat" Brewster, a small boy in Banff at the end of the nineteenth century, the son of a pioneer dairyman, says Twin frequently used sign language; and Moore and McDougall obviously heard William with different ears.)

In the summer of 1896 two prospectors named Temple and Smith set out for the far side of the Divide and ran into difficulties. Wilcox records that an accident resulted in their being separated on either side of a fast-flowing stream. Smith wandered for almost two weeks in the wilderness. He'd just about given up all hope of life when he heard a locomotive whistle. Shouting to a section crew on the far side of the Bow River, Smith found safety, but no one had heard the fate of Temple. William Twin's tracking ability resolved the mystery. In Banff a rescue party for Temple formed up:

> William, with that wonderful power that the Indians alone seem to possess, of observing the faintest signs, followed the track of the rescued prospector up Healy's Creek, over the Simpson Pass to the Vermilion River, and thence to the place where the fatal raft had been wrecked. One of the horses was found here, and then, crossing the river, he took up the trail of the other prospector. With marvellous skill he led the way, even where the hard ground or solid rock preserved no apparent footmarks. In one place he crossed a river on a log-jam, saying, as he pointed to the smooth logs: 'Me see him trail—he go here—he go here,' and in fact footprints appeared in the sand on the other side. The trail led them in two days more to the stage road on the Columbia, and they surmised that Temple had reached safety, as indeed was the case.

William had followed an ancient trail, one the Kootenay and Stoney had used for centuries. Eleven kilometres west of Banff, near where the Stoney forded the Bow River to its south side and thence to Healy Creek, Simpson Pass, and the good hunting of the Vermilion, Mitchell, and Kootenay valleys stood the Sawback Section House where a century ago my grandfather Dave White became CPR section man. En route to and from the hunting grounds, small family hunting parties used to stop in for tea and conversation. Mark Poucette and his family, Dan Wildman, the Twins, William and Joshua, the Hunters: all became friends. The friendships formed then led to a complicated relationship between my family in Banff and the Morley Stoney.

Both Stoney and Kootenay had continued hunting the mountain valleys, but by the turn of the twentieth century new concepts again endangered their traditions. Walking Buffalo (George McLean) told Marius Barbeau in the early 1920s that the two tribes had been excellent friends. The Kootenay, he explained, were wont to hunt bison with the Stoney on the eastern slope of the Rockies—while bison were still for the hunting—and the Stoney visited the western slopes and the Columbia Valley to hunt mountain game with the Kootenay. The governments of Alberta and British Columbia, as well as the federal authority, he indicated, were opposed to the friendship, trying to keep the two peoples apart. Walking Buffalo explained the feelings of the Stoney:

> The Chiefs of the Stonies and the Kootenays, over at Windermere, made an appointment every year to meet again. It was to decide whether the Kootenays and Stonies were to continue to visit each other. After a while they decided that we had to stop from going over. It was because the government thought we killed off the game when we visited them. It was the reason why they stopped us.

He continued his lamentation by saying his people used to feel free, but they no longer felt at home in the land. Stoney women had married Kootenay men and moved to the Columbia Valley; family ties were severed. The fencing of the land alienated traditional Indian campsites, and they could not obtain permission from the landowners to use the old campsites, and "this used to be our country."

The same month the railroad connected eastern Canada to the Pacific, November, 1885, the Government of Canada created a twenty-six square kilometre reserve around the hot springs at Banff which would become Canada's first national park. The American painter of Indians, George Catlin, conceived national parks as a way of protecting traditional Plains Indian life against encroaching industrial civilization. His concept ironically turned against the Stoney. In 1886 the Department of the Interior in Ottawa sent to Banff a biologist, W. F. Whitcher, who reported: "Large game and fish, once various and plentiful in this mountainous region, are now scattered and comparatively scarce. Skin-hunters, dynamiters, and netters, with Indians, wolves and foxes, have committed sad havoc." (Whitcher places Indians among predators.) "The Indians," he added, "have this season still further diminished" the "fragmentary bands" of "wary mountain sheep and stupid goats" frequenting the mountaintops, and he blamed "the decimation of fluvial trout in these waters'' on ''giant powder, nets, and the improvidence of Indian fishing.'' The Whitcher report led to the first wildlife regulation and protection policies in the National Park, principally to assure stocks for hunters and sportsmen, since he seems to have thought the National Park was a Canadian equivalent to an English gentleman's hunting preserve. Famine in the early 1880s obliged the Stoney and other peoples of the mountain frontier to seek protein wherever it browsed, and if they sought it in the mountains, where they had found it for generations, who can blame them?

In mid-November, 1896, a Stoney party, the family of Chief Hector Crawler, was returning from a hunting expedition to the Kootenay River region when a metre and a half of snow blanketed the Bow Valley in a two-day period. Near the Bow Ford, after a terrible trip down Healy Creek, the Crawlers took to the railroad line for their hard walk to Morley. A locomotive smashed into the group. The chief's brother, George Crawler, managed to herd the women and children into the drifts, but the chief was injured and many of their horses were killed. The Banff newspaper, *The Crag and Canyon,* retelling the story twenty years later, said Chief Crawler ''was a mad Indian and vowed to shoot the engineer on sight, a vow he would undoubtedly have kept had not the railway men deemed it prudent to seek a change of climate.''

In 1907 the families of Sampson Beaver and Silas Abraham, members of the Wesley Band of Stoney, were camped on the Kootenay Plains, the Katoonda Tinda or Windy Plains on the North Saskatchewan River, adjacent to the old Kootenay Indian trail leading from the plains to Howse Pass and the Columbia River. Into their camp that summer came horses from the south, one of them bearing Yahe-Weha, Mountain Woman, their affectionate name for Mary Schäffer, who had continued visiting the Rockies after her first trip to Lake Louise when she had met William Twin. Thirty years after Treaty #7, the North Saskatchewan Stoney still lived, trapped, and hunted in the mountains, and the national parks had not extended north from Banff or south from Jasper to take in their hunting region. The Ram, Clearwater, and Brazeau River drainages were their backyard and frontyard, and they knew the valleys well. To the north of the Windy Plains, several days' travel, Sampson Beaver said, was a large lake, Chaba Imne, and the adventurers were keen to seek it. Sampson provided them with a map they held and cherished for a year. Mary Schäffer's account in *Old Indian Trails* provides a memorable portrait of Stoney humour:

> Beginning, I said: 'Silas, do you really let your squaw saddle and pack your horses?' 'Sure.' (How well he had learned English!) 'And let her fix the tepee-poles and put up the tepee?' 'Yes.' 'And get the wood, and cook, and tan the skins?' 'Yes, sure!' (He was growing impatient at so much quizzing.) The time seemed ripe for some missionary work which was perceptibly needed along more lines than one, and every one had stopped to listen.

> 'Now, Silas,' I said impressively, 'you should be like the white men, you should do the work for your squaw. *We* do not put up our tepees or pack our horses or cut the wood, our men do that.' Taking his pipe from his mouth and inspecting me from head to foot leisurely, he said, 'You lazy!'

More remote from the railways and the ways of settlement than their kin at Morley, the members of Abraham's band would follow their old customs for several more decades. Finally the pincers of civilization would close on the northern band of Wesleys too.

Yahe-Weha and her companions returned the following year, to follow Sampson's map to Chaba Imne, the now-famous Maligne Lake of Jasper National Park.

As Banff and its neighbouring national parks of Yoho, Jasper, and Kootenay grew, the government forbade hunting in them for the Stoney (and others too)—whether at Morley or by the North Saskatchewan River. The vast size of the parks made policing them nigh impossible before the development of the warden service, but within a generation the Stoney—and most non-Indians too—respected the game regulations of the parks. In 1921 Jimmy Simpson, a Banff outfitter and hunting guide, wrote J. B. Harkin, the Commissioner of National Parks and the North West Game Act, suggesting that Indians seriously menaced the perpetuation of wildlife in the mountains. Harkin agreed that "the Indian question is one of the most serious ones we have in connection with wild life protection," but denied it was a problem in the parks: "This of course does not apply to any extent to the parks because I think that the Indians have been taught to recognize the sanctity of parks boundaries. We certainly do not make any exception in their favour and do not propose to do so."

Alienation of hunting lands, through the development of parks—national as well as provincial parks, like Mount Assiniboine and Kananaskis—and wilderness areas in Alberta, forest reserves, and ranching, gas extraction plants, pipelines, and highway construction, has further depleted the hunting areas Treaty #7 guaranteed the Stoneys.

Mrs Hunter with Chief John Hunter, Chiniki Band, Stoney, circa 1915, in regalia for an Indian Days parade.
Photo by Byron Harmon, courtesy the Whyte Museum of the Canadian Rockies.

8

Indian Days

In the summer of 1889 torrential downpours washed out the Canadian Pacific Railway's line in the Rockies, keeping the visitors at the Banff Springs Hotel in Banff longer than they anticipated. The two-year-old Banff Springs Hotel—a grand hotel even then, if only sixty or so rooms—tried to keep its guests amused, but when it became obvious that track crews were moving slowly, and no trains would depart east or west from the resort town for a week and a half, the guests turned a mite squirrelly.

The hotel manager, W. L. Mathews, contacting Tom Wilson, who'd moseyed around the Rockies eight years or so, asked him what to do. Tom, a member of the 1881 and 1882 railroad surveying parties who'd stayed on in Banff after the CPR's completion in 1885 to become the region's first packer-outfitter, suggested he and Dave White would talk to their Stoney friends and try to arrange some entertainment for the stranded tourists. Tom rode his pony sixty-five kilometres to Morley to talk to the Stoney, who readily agreed to ride up to Banff.

Two hundred and fifty Stoney arrived in Banff in a couple of days, some of them by horse, their hide tepees carried in the still traditional horse travois, but many arrived by wagons, creaking and groaning up the tote road the CPR developed for its railroad construction six years earlier. On the way, the tribe camped for a night at what came to be called Indian Flats, just east of the railroad's division point of Canmore, an old campsite for the Stoney. From its informal beginning, Banff Indian Days became first an important festival for the Morley Stoney, then a gathering for other Mountain Peoples as well—Stoney from the North Saskatchewan River, Kootenay from the Columbia Valley, Sarcee from near Calgary.

The Stoney made their first Indian Days encampment beside the Bow River below Bow Falls, a traditional campsite beneath Mount Rundle's cliffs and Tunnel Mountain's sheer wall, a short ride or walk up to the Banff Springs Hotel to entertain the guests. The Stoney stayed in the resort area for about a week, and the hotel management, the Banff business community, and the Stoney had a great time. The new festival offered an unusual opportunity for the Stoney, then twelve years on the reserve, to practise and enjoy their Indianness. Horse races, foot races, the tug'o'war, parades, dancing—and an opportunity for the "white savages" (as Walking Buffalo would later call them) to visit the romantic, scarcely known, tepee homes of the once-nomadic Stoney. The sporting events continued to be the centre of Banff Indian Days, and within several years the popularity of Indian Days required a larger site, both for the camp and for the activities. The new location was the flats near Minnehappa, the waterfall north of Banff at the foot of Cascade Mountain, where townsfolk had made and abandoned a racetrack.

The foregoing version of the events, Tom Wilson's version, is contradicted by Dave White's recorded statements of 1938. As a recently-appointed section man for the CPR in 1889, he knew no washout disrupted service in the Rockies that year, and he saw only occasional Stoney hunting parties.

He believed Indian Days grew from more informal occasions. Banffites held their sports days on the twenty-fourth of May (Queen Victoria's birthday) and July first (Dominion Day, the anniversary of Canada's confederation), and Stoney men, women, and children would occasionally join in the competitions. As a merchant on Banff Avenue after 1894 he was quite familiar with all the comings and goings in the town. More and more people from Morley came up to participate in the sports throughout the later 1890s, and by 1900 horse races between Stoney and Banff equestrians were held on Bear Street, close by the corrals where Bill Peyto, Jim Simpson, Fred Ballard, and other outfitters and packers had located their stables and tack sheds. By 1902 whole families were arriving, and some 200 Stoney made an encampment at their traditional camp site near Minnehappa, the waterfall on Cascade Mountain. Wilson's story, he said, was typical Tom—good story-telling.

The McDougall Mission at Morley, concerned with the Stoneys' welfare, their spiritual lives and redemption, little heeded the Stoneys' deep-rooted traditions. Forcefully expressing his disdain for such traditions as the Sundance, forbidding participation in such rites, believing Stoney song, music, and dance to be expressions of an alien religion, John McDougall, his biographer says, "condemned the pow-wow and sun dance with their tom-tom, paint, feathers and incantations, as tending to maintain pagan worship and practice. Indeed the Stoney Indians, through his ministrations, legislated in their Councils against even the making of drums until they were not allowed to be kept on the Reserves. However, he felt there were sufficient safeguards at the [Calgary] Stampede and the [Banff Indian Days] Pageants to protect the natives; the amusement would relieve the monotony of life on the Reserve, while the knowledge obtained would be beneficial to them all."

The mission and the residential school the federal government established on the Morley Reserve were placing barriers between the Stoney and their "savage past." Even today older Indians resent their school experience, believing they emerged from it as neither Indians nor white people. The school, they say, made them ashamed of their language, embarrassed by their past; and the students obtained few skills with which to cope with a white world. Indian Days at Banff allowed them to be proudly Stoney, to revel in a noble past, apologizing to no one for the grandeur of their costumes, the sublimity of their music, the richness of their culture.

When the summer encampment moved to the foot of Cascade Mountain, it lay near the animal paddocks where the National Park maintained a small herd of bison. By 1900 bison had vanished to all but memory for older Stoney. By 1930 the animal that once provided the foundation of the lives of the

Plains People—and most Stoney had been Plains People for generations before they moved into the mountains—had become so rare that grandfathers would take their grandchildren by hand and walk the kilometre over to the bison stockade to show the young ones the animal's magnificence, and tell them stories of hunting bison in the old days. If the Stoney did not come to Banff, a writer for *The Crag and Canyon* stated, "the rising generation would not see the 'mustoosch' (cattle) of their fathers' stories and the narratives of wonderful hunting would not mean so much to them. Thus the annual trip of the Stoneys to Banff assists in keeping alive the precious stories and legends to that race."

The mountain fastnesses had for a century or more resounded with the most important Stoney ritual, the Sundance they had brought with them from the plains. The Stoney never held Sundances during Banff Indian Days, refusing to engage in a religious rite before a curious and unheeding audience. The upper Bow Valley held sacred significance for many older Stoney who had performed rites among the peaks in the past. A *Crag and Canyon* story in 1936 explained how the Stoney propitiated an evil spirit in their traditional religion by making "little personal sacrifices...for his pleasure at certain places in the mountains—at the Hoodoos, for one, the braves would leave pieces of tobacco, treasured pipes and other offerings to the bad spirit, believing that they would thus gain favor from him. Thus at the yearly gathering [for the Sundance] there would be dances and sacrifices in this spirit for his kindness in having spared them through the past winter, and other dances and sacrifices to gain his favor through the coming winter."

During the 1920s the National Park administration donated three bison to the Indian Days camp each summer. The elders seized the opportunity to demonstrate their butchery skills to the younger band members. In 1926 a *Crag and Canyon* writer reported how skillfully the Stoney cut up a four-year-old bull:

> Dan Wildman, Judas Hunter, Mark Poucette, and Paul Twoyoungman were soon busy with adroit strokes separating the hide from the carcass. It was soon evident to the bystanders that the Indian butcher's methods are very different from the white man's. First, the Indian wants as much blood as possible left in the meat. Secondly he does not cut it against the grain, but slices it off in slabs, following the muscle and tissues, being very careful not to cut any more arteries than possible.
>
> Their knowledge of the anatomy of the buffalo was a revelation to the onlookers, and in forty minutes from the time the shot was fired, every vestige of what had once been a lordly 1,500-pound four-year-old buffalo bull had entirely disappeared. This feat was accomplished with one axe and four knives, without the aid of any of the modern butcher's implements for hoisting, etc., exactly as did their ancestors in centuries past.

Because of our family's involvement with Banff Indian Days, I spent nearly every afternoon of Indian Days at the Indian Grounds in the 1940s watching races and rodeo events. I spent as many evenings at the concerts of traditional song and dance the Stoney presented at the grandstand on the edge of the athletic grounds at the Banff Springs Hotel. I watched nearly every parade. More specially, I was allowed to call upon old David and Mrs Bearspaw in their tepee, which held the place of honour in the encampment the Stoney erected just north of Banff. Mr and Mrs Bearspaw, or Mr and Mrs George McLean (Walking Buffalo, whose medicine-man costume of hides, his headdress of bison horns, and his necklace of claws sufficed to awe anyone, even those more sophisticated than a five-year-old lad), or George Kaquitts, or members of the Twoyoungman family: we called upon them all, and I learned early to love the pleasing scents of sweetgrass and poplar smoke, buckskin and earth odours, more intimately in the Indian Grounds encampment than anywhere else.

My father was official starter for the novelty horse races one year, and invited me to join him in the infield to watch the events from the best vantage point. Part of me believes the races mildly exploited their competitors, but the entrants enjoyed them thoroughly, and the calico crowd of Indians and visitors alike thought them terrific. A few horse races were pure: starting line flag, twice around the course, first man across winning. The novelty races held more fascination. The Cigar Race, for instance: light your cigar upon the signal, mount your horse, first man across the finish line—his cigar still lit—wins. The Pie Race tormented its entrants: at the drop of the flag each racer ate a whole pie—usually apple—then mounted his steed for a loop. Some of those kids (contestants were usually in their late teens) must never have had a pie to themselves before; came a whole pie their way, the race obliged their eating it in thirty seconds! The Slow Race posed tricky knots for a seven-year-old to comprehend: in its topsy-turvy world, the horse counted, not the rider, for the riders exchanged horses before the race began. The owner of the last horse to cross the finish line was the winner. He had to ride dead out on a strange horse to force his own horse to run last. Lewis Carroll would have understood. Such races had a curious origin. The Stoney themselves keenly competed as horsemen in dead-out races across the Morley Flats at home. In 1936 *The Crag and Canyon* traced the roots of the novelty races to the first gathering in 1889:

> Pony races, foot races, and every kind of sport known to the Indians were organized, with braves and squaws participating in the events. Any contest suggested by a hotel guest was immediately tried on the straight race track of the day which has since become the main road to the Banff Springs Hotel.

In the 1940s most Stoney, even those who came to Banff from as far away as Nordegg near the North Saskatchewan River, arrived by horse-drawn democrats. Families of grandparents, parents, kids; tepees and all the costumes piled in the back; other horses strung behind, tail-tied one to the other: a caravan of unique ancestry.

Some races featured the democrats. The horses would stand ten or fifteen feet in front of the wagons, out of harness. On the starting signal teams of racers would yoke the horses, get them in place, set the double tree and single trees, get the bridles into the horses' mouths and grab the traces, snapping the whip to get the rigs going. Nothing like the Calgary Stampede Chuckwagon Races: the harnessing activity at Indian Days took place before our eyes, twenty to thirty feet away. In the bustle of getting teams underway, some racers made shortcuts in the harnessing. On at least one occasion I remember the horses suddenly found their load lighter because the democrat had come loose and careered off the course. A chagrined racer dashed across the open infield to cut off his team and recover it as it crossed the finish line so he could lead it back to his democrat, hitch it up, and try to sneak quietly off the track to avoid the derision of his neighbours who had seen too clearly the effects of his careless harnessing.

My aunt, Catharine Whyte, provides a wonderful story about the sturdiness of what she called a "rickerty" democrat. In 1947 George McLean had not felt well at Indian Days, so he and his wife took a holiday in the mountains. From Morley they drove their democrat to Rocky Mountain House, about two hundred and fifty kilometres north, then turned west to Nordegg, the Kootenay Plains, and the Banff-Jasper Highway, another one hundred and sixty kilometres, fifty of them on rough trail not improved in a hundred years of use, then a hundred and thirty kilometres on to Banff, stopping in for a meal with Pete and Catharine before teaming the last sixty-five back to Morley. In a letter to her mother, Catharine records some of the lore George related during the meal.

> He told us a lot about the old Indian trails. How they used to go up what is now Johnston's Canyon, across to Baker Lake and the head of the Little Red Deer, up the Pipestone and to the Siffleur (which they called the 'trail of the deep snow': their names are so much more appropriate than ours) and then to Kootenay Plains. Johnston's Canyon was called White Goat Little River.

The rope George used to hold the extra horses interested my uncle, she adds:

> Some would have tied it to the back of the wagon which might have been dangerous had the horses bolted on the highway, or they could have held it in the hand which becomes very tiring. George just sat on the end of the rope and if anything should happen it would pull out and he had his hands free.

In the afternoons of Indian Days the rodeo followed the horse racing. A small but complete rodeo: bareback and saddle bronc bucking, brahma bull riding, barrel racing, calf-roping, steer decoration, wild cow milking, and a wild horse race. Bleachers at one side of the field provided good visibility for spectators. Only a wovewire fence screened the action, and more than once a bucking horse plummeted from the sky toward the eyes of a little kid who, petrified, found he could barely move his legs fast enough to flee disaster imminent. I learned early to appreciate the skills of rodeo clowns; their seemingly capricious diversion of the sharp horns of enraged brahma bulls from stunned riders, their jesting to fill in the lulls inevitable in rodeo as horses balked in the chutes. People who think Indians lack a sense of humour should have seen the Indian rodeo clowns exhibit both humour and skill in their ploys.

The Stoney kids and the Banff kids engaged in a special kind of horse trading during Banff Indian Days. I thought it unique to our generation, trading a bicycle for a horse for a day or an afternoon, but, talking to townsfolk of an older generation than mine, I found the practice common since the days after the First World War.

From the late 1920s on, the Stoney and their friends from other tribes presented concerts and pageants at a grandstand the Banff Springs Hotel erected on the fringe of its athletic grounds. John Murray Gibbon, the CPR's public relations officer, who loved pageants and Canadian folklore, allied his passions with CPR promotion. The skill of the artists intrigued me: a five-year-old hoop dancer could rotate two hoops on each arm, one on each thigh, one about his neck; chicken dancers could emulate each antic movement of a prairie chicken's mating dance, the insinuating rhythms of Indian drummers and their staccato keening echoed from the rock parapets of the hotel Gibbon called "the great stone tepee." Whip dancers snapped their riatas a few metres from the audience. Most intriguingly, two teen-aged boys imitated animal sounds with their own voices: dog growls, wolf howls, coyote yips, cat snarls, then, in finale, a tumult of the menagerie as cats, dogs, and beasts of the wild caterwauled in mayhem.

The performers diluted some of the older songs and dances, shortening the material, sweetening it for performance, joking and jesting around its edges, but most of it remained authentic, accurate—if abbreviated—rite. Those performances must have been, if not unique, then very rare. In few other places then could a non-Indian hear intimations of the powwow. For purposes of the parades, the concerts, and the joys of Banff Indian Days, the Stoney and their neighbours kept their costumes intact and maintained the links with a vital past.

The last afternoon of Banff Indian Days, Sunday, the Stoney opened their tepees to the public, and held competitions in the rodeo infield. By then, a century to a century and a half after the last Stoney relied upon archery for a meal, only the festival event summoned marksmanship with a bow and arrow, and the shooters frequently missed the target completely, not just the bull's-eye. Fletchers still made excellent arrows, willow bows strung with sinew still demanded strength, but life or death depended not on good eye, steady hand, or the knowledge of release timing. As comical were the efforts of the men in the tepee pitching contest. The Stoney had not forgotten how to pitch their beautiful tabernacles. (Many of them still pitch tepees beside their Morley residences for summer homes.) The women usually formed the tripod the other poles lean upon, knew the diameter of the circle to support their particular tent, and adeptly achieved the form in minutes. Men, however, competed in the event. Lean-to poles collapsed, the shroud refused to lie gracefully upon the frame, and they'd have to tug it into place carefully so as not to distress the fabric. Sometimes the tepee would lie lopped about the ground like a short lady's too-long petticoats, if the circle were too small. All the while the Stoney spectators would exhort the competitors, ''Hanjumbo!'' In little kids' imitative fashion, we also shouted the word, the Stoney standing beside us giggling, then asking if we knew what we were saying. They told us it meant ''Hurry up!''

By the late 1930s the popularity of Banff Indian Days with the Stoney caused the government department responsible for Indians to order a restriction on the number visiting Banff for the festival. The Department of Mines and Resources (the portfolio incorporated both Indian Affairs and National Parks) ruled that only one hundred and fifty Stoney could trek to Banff: the others must stay to tend the Reserve's haying and farming operations. (The Calgary Stampede first, then Banff Indian Days following a week later: many Stoney were away from home more than two weeks in July.) The Stoney replied they all came or no one came. They all came. The Stoney held firm to their convictions, and little changed for three decades.

In 1947 Mark Poucette arrived at Banff without a tepee. Running into my aunt and uncle, he asked if he might stay with them, but Pete, remembering a tepee stored in their garage, promised Mark he'd deliver it to the grounds. A wind had arisen, so they also left Mark a rope so he could tether the tepee to the ground to prevent its blowing over. Mark left for Morley a day early, and someone told Pete and Catharine he'd left the tepee behind. In a letter to her mother Catharine completed the story, saying, ''We forgot to go down until late Sunday night and sure enough there was the tepee and the rope lying with one loop around the end of a tepee pole. Apparently no one watching it, and though it had been there over 24 hours, not even the rope had been borrowed. I wonder how long it would have stayed unmolested among that many white people.''

A Banff group headed by Norman Luxton worked strenuously on arrangements for the festival. Luxton, an adventurer who had crossed the Pacific in a West Coast Indian canoe with one other man, was publisher of *The Crag and*

Canyon. A long-time friend of the Stoney, he had married David McDougall's daughter, who grew up on the Morley Reserve. He remained the mainstay of the organization for the festival's early years, raising and disbursing funds and working with the Stoney to set dates and solve transportation problems. At the end of the Second World War, Luxton handed the reins to others, and Claude Brewster, the son of a Banff pioneer outfitter and an outfitter himself, took them, and looked after most of the arrangements for the next two decades. Each participating family received a stipend for coming to Banff, another stipend for erecting a tepee and performing in the concerts. Local businesses donated food for the camp and prizes for competitions, members of the town's service clubs managed the gate, and kept the rodeo on schedule. Local people judged the costumes the Stoney wore for the parades, and again there were prizes from local donors. The administration of Banff National Park, frequently engaged in culling elk from the park's herds, provided eight or ten carcases for a supply of meat.

In the late 1960s and early 1970s changing attitudes and varying cultural demands began to fray the edges of the festival. The Banff Kiwanis Club took over from Claude Brewster after the 1968 festival, and for a couple of years the Kiwanis threw their enthusiasm into the event, reinvigorating it, increasing the stipends for participation in the parades, for erecting a tepee, and for the rodeo events. But the raison d'être for the festival was weakening. No longer did the Stoney hitch up a team for a two-day democrat trip to Banff; most owned cars by then. Fewer Stoney brought horses to Banff for the parades, and the spectacular sight of many chiefs on horseback retreated to memory. The Stoney were exploring their own cultural traditions at home in Morley.

The Banff Indian Days committee found getting stock to Banff for the rodeo events increasingly difficult, and maintaining the rodeo facilities was beyond its resources. Cultural events, however, interested Banff's visitors more than did the rodeo. Claude Brewster, observing the situation, succinctly summed it up: "Most Indians today," he said, "prefer to be cowboys." For a year the Banff committee ran the cultural events and the Stoney ran the rodeo. The local organizers brought in some "mean stock" from the Calgary Stampede in 1969, and introduced the Indian Days Dollar, designed by Banff sculptor Charlie Beil, to raise funds to reward the participants. The Kiwanis Club manufactured the coins, which it then distributed to local merchants who could use them in lieu of change for purchases. The coins could be redeemed for legal tender, but most visitors kept them as souvenirs, and the proceeds went to paying the expenses for Indian Days. In 1970 the rodeo aspect of Indian Days disappeared. Without the rodeo, many Stoney decided to stay home.

Rising Indian consciousness in the 1970s, bred in such incidents as the Wounded Knee and Alcatraz occupations in the United States, led the Stoney to perceive events like Banff Indian Days as a spectacle where they put themselves on show. Banff's visitors had also changed; in earlier decades they stayed in the Rockies for a week or more after a long train trip brought them to Banff. After the completion of the Trans-Canada Highway in 1962, visitors came by car, staying for a day or two only before they rolled on. If Banff Indian Days coincided with their visit, they might take in the events, but they rarely scheduled journeys to be in Banff for them. No one bears the blame for the festival's demise: it lost its significance for both its participants and its spectators in a more rushing world that developed. Only the older Stoney, who had anticipated Banff Indian Days more keenly than Christmas, sustained a lively interest in the events. The income from the Indian Days dollars resulted in some fattening of the budget, but the money went only so far. The organizers gave honoraria to the first people to erect tepees, while the Stoney felt that any family putting up a tepee should receive an honorarium. Disgruntlement developed.

The Kiwanis found that the costs of the festival were draining its resources, so the service club handed local arrangements over to a new group. With the encouragement of the manager of the Banff Springs Hotel, Ivor Petrak, a new committee was formed whose members were Wally Dowhaniuk, Bus Rivett, George Mandryk, John Pawluk, Don Henderson, Jim Santa Lucia, Gordon DeBoice, Jim Parker, and Craig Rothwell. Many of the members had worked with the Stoney before. In 1971 the Stoney, like their predecessors in the 1930s, grew angry when they did not all receive pay for taking part in the events. They announced they were boycotting Banff Indian Days, since they felt they weren't getting a fair deal. They planned a competing festival for Morley and invited other tribes to join them. Cancelling the rodeo was another issue: the Banff committee had found it expensive and troublesome, and it interested only the Stoney. The Banff community vigorously tried to keep the festival alive. Robert Smallboy, Chief of a Cree band that had left its reserve to return to the land and live in a traditional fashion near the Kootenay Plains on the North Saskatchewan River, responded quickly to an invitation the Association extended him, and brought his people to Banff where they set up an encampment for the week.

In 1972 some of the Stoney returned to Banff, along with Cree from the north, Sarcee from Calgary, Blackfoot from Gleichen, Kootenay from the west. The Lieutenant-Governor of Alberta, the Honourable Ralph Steinhauer, born in Morley in 1905, who for thirty-four years served as a councillor of the Saddle Lake Reserve, opened the events. It seemed that Banff Indian Days would endure. The mix of competitions and cultural events seemed appealing. But in 1976 Bill McLean, Chief of the Bearspaw Band and a son of Walking Buffalo, independently sought the approval of the Minister of Northern Affairs to hold a rodeo during Banff Indian Days if the Indian Days Committee agreed. The representatives of the other participating tribes, the

Sarcee, Cree, and Blackfoot who had continued Indian Days when the Stoney boycotted it, opposed the rodeo. So did the park superintendent. The Stoney cried foul; no rodeo occurred.

After the 1978 Banff Indian Days the Indian Days Association wearied of the job, the deficits, the thanklessness. Three of its most vigorous members announced their retirement. The Stoney, offered a chance to run the show themselves, weren't interested either. Banff Indian Days dwindled to nothingness.

No longer do tepees cluster for a July week in the Rockies; no more do curls of poplar smoke rise from the elegant cone tents by Minnehappa. The flaps are closed. We all, I believe, are poorer for the festival's demise. The landscape has lost a human element it harboured for many centuries. Few Trans-Canada travellers recognize how ancient a trail they make their way upon as they drive from Calgary to Banff. The valleys seem lonelier for the absence of the soft tread of the Kootenay, the Stoney, the Shuswap, the Sarcee.

All Our Yesterdays

A Stoney medicine man used to walk west from the Morley Reserve to a great cliff above Lac des Arcs. He'd climb the cliff on his spirit quest, and once atop it, the Bow Valley spread before him, he would meditate and ponder. From time to time one of the little spirits of the place would come and talk to him. One day in the 1950s, the little man and he were in conversation, and the little man told him he was going to leave that place. There was a highway coming up that side of the valley, so he was going to go up to the North Saskatchewan River way. And that's the way it happened. The Stoney went back to that place, but he never saw that little man again.

My uncle Pete used to remark how grateful we ought to be in Banff that the Morley Reserve lay across the Bow Valley midway between Banff and Calgary. Nothing else, he thought, could so assuredly block Calgary's westward growth. Surely and inevitably, Alberta's transformation from a rural society to an urban society in the twenty years between 1960 and 1980 resulted in transformations in Stoney society too.

Increasing demands for energy in the 1970s in Alberta and British Columbia again altered the lives of the native peoples of the Rocky Mountains. A dam on the Peace River in northeastern British Columbia blocked the old routes of the Beaver Indians who had hunted and trapped in the region for more than two centuries.

Farther south, in the Central Rockies, the construction of a dam on the North Saskatchewan River, near where a group of the Wesleys had lived for nearly a century, resulted in turmoil in their lives. They, like the Indians of the northern forest, had relied upon hunting for their subsistence economy. At a remove from the travel routes intersecting the Rockies by the Yellowhead, Kicking Horse, and Crowsnest Passes, the Wesleys had blithely ignored most of the twentieth century, subsisting on game, and earning a small income by trapping and hunting. They had annually travelled south to Banff for Indian Days; once or twice a year they'd ridden into Rocky Mountain House for supplies and staples. But, until oil- and gas-seeking seismic crews arrived with their equipment, then engineers looking for a dam site, the only people they had seen were occasional adventurers rafting on the river in the summers, hunting parties in the autumns headed into the valleys of the Brazeau, Ram, or Clearwater Rivers, or from time to time an automobile caravan proceeding along the valley by the old fur trade route.

In the late 1960s the dam builders arrived. The new century arrived with a jolt, and attractive–if soul-destroying–urban living wrenched the northern Wesley band from their land-oriented lives. Not provided a reserve by any treaty, the Wesleys had happily ignored the confinements restraining their southern kin. When the land developed economic potential, the governments of Canada and Alberta immediately began to consider where to create a reserve for the Wesleys. Where the Bighorn River flows into the North Saskatchewan River, the band obtained a reserve. An old cemetery, including the graves of Silas Abraham and his children, had to be moved upstream to the edges of the Kootenay Plains before the reservoir inundated the site. A new road, connecting Nordegg to the Icefield Parkway running from Banff to Jasper, intersected the reserve. Within a decade alcoholism began fraying the once well-woven fabric of the people's lives; they became wards of the welfare system.

Construction of the Trans-Canada Highway in the late 1950s (the highway the little man had foreseen) intersected the Morley Reserve. Within a decade increasing tourism in the Rockies demanded twinning the highway to four lanes. The new political fervour of the era resulted in a Stoney threat to barricade the highway during a holiday weekend before the government of Alberta listened to their demands for compensating land grants to offset the inconvenience created by the swath of highway running through their land. The younger councillors and chiefs—many of whom had settled into lives as ranchers—wanted more range land lower in the Bow Valley, but the elders, perhaps romantically, held out for wooded country to the north of the reserve where they thought the hunting was good.

Exploration for natural gas in the land taken into the reserve resulted in a windfall for the Morley Stoney. The land transfer from the Alberta Government included mineral rights to the land—unusual in a provincial land transfer where mineral rights traditionally remain with the Crown—and the Stoney soon found their tribe had the largest income of any Indian reserve in Canada. With a unique opportunity to take economic development into their own hands, the Stoney cautiously but earnestly started to consider the sort of developments they wished to undertake. First on their agenda was housing: many of the 2,000 Stoney had lived in small log cabins for most of their eighty to ninety years on the reserve. They purchased an established ranch adjacent to the reserve. For a period they used it as a rodeo school—fulfilling their yearning to be among the best of cowboys. Within a decade they turned it into a necessary facility for their lives, an alcohol and drug detoxification centre. The tribe built an arena and the Morley Wesleys built the Chief Chiniki Rodeo Centre—because entertainment facilities on the reserve are meagre.

In another accomplishment, the Wesley Band at Morley purchased the facilities the YMCA had developed as Camp Chief Hector, and for a period ran the Stoney Wilderness School in the old buildings, providing opportunities for the elders of the tribe to pass on their traditional skills to both the younger Stoney and interested outsiders. In the early 1980s the Wesley Band replaced the old facilities with the Nakodah Lodge, a combined research facility and gathering place where it hopes to preserve its culture in a museum and transmit it to the oncoming generation. Elsewhere on the reserve the Tribal Council established a restaurant, a gift shop to sell the handcrafts of Stoney and other Indians, and facilities for other stores and a laundry in the community so the Stoney would no longer have to drive to the not-so-nearby towns of Cochrane, Exshaw, and Canmore.

Indian reserves in Canada frequently have a symbiotic relationship with nearby non-Indian communities, and most of the funds given to the Indians have not remained long on the reserves. The Stoney hope to keep their own economy rolling with their own developments, keeping their money on the reserve.

Nearer Calgary, the Sarcee also obtained new funds in the late 1970s, and built, among other facilities, a museum shaped in the outline of a beaver, visibly reminding them of their heritage, the time generations ago in the northern forest when their nation was crossing the lake and the child saw the monster under the ice that rose up and sundered them into the Beaver Indians and the Sarcee. Few in number—there are no more than a thousand Sarcee—they proudly revere their woodland past while they sustain themselves as ranchers and farmers.

On the other side of the mountains, in the Rocky Mountain Trench, the Kootenay, few in number, are still the horsemen they have been for two and a half centuries. Rarely do the once-knowledgeable Kootenay, the ones who understood the geography of the Rockies better than any other Indian nation, cross the mountains these days. In the demise of Banff's Indian Days, only an occasional rodeo at Morley attracts the Kootenay to cross the mountains to the land that was once their realm.

To the north of the Kootenay live a few of the Rocky Mountain Shuswap. Another dam, Mica Dam on the Columbia River, greatly enlarged a lake that recalls their nineteenth-century chief in its name—Kinbasket.

The acts of enclosure are now almost complete. The mountain national parks—Yoho, Kootenay, Jasper, Banff, and Waterton—have grown, and, adjacent to them, the provincial parks at Mount Assiniboine and Mount Robson in British Columbia, and, along the Kananaskis River in Alberta, Kananaskis Provincial Park and Kananaskis Country. No longer can a nomad subsist on mountain routes.

The route to respect for the Mountain Indians has been arduous and long. Romanticized a century ago for their nobility, the Indians believed the fables too, and, in their failing to live up to an idealized image of themselves, felt duress and pain. In poverty and disease, feeling misunderstanding and prejudice, they have struggled to come to terms with their past and their present. Now, a century after the reserves were established on both sides of the Rockies, they are beginning—but just beginning—to feel they have a heritage to preserve and to share. They'll save their culture, but most of them are in a struggle against time to salvage their almost forgotten spirits.

Portfolio

Panoramic view of the Banff Indian Days camp, circa 1910.
Photo by Byron Harmon, courtesy the Whyte Museum of the Canadian Rockies.

Camp, early winter, 1887 or 1888.
Photo by Boorne and May, courtesy the Whyte Museum of the Canadian Rockies.

Stoney boys with playhouse tepees, Kootenay Plains, circa 1906. Indian children learned the traditions of their tribe in play activities.
Photo by Elliott Barnes, courtesy the Whyte Museum of the Canadian Rockies.

Joe Stevens, circa 1910.
Portrait by Byron Harmon, courtesy the Whyte Museum of the Canadian Rockies.

Mr and Mrs Morley Beaver and child, Stoney, circa 1910.
Photo by Byron Harmon, courtesy the Whyte Museum of the Canadian Rockies.

Stoney horse race at Morley, circa 1910.
Photo by Elliott Barnes, courtesy the Whyte Museum of the Canadian Rockies.

Mrs Tom Kaquitts scraping a hide, Banff Indian Days, circa 1920.
Photo by Byron Harmon, courtesy the Whyte Museum of the Canadian Rockies.

A Sarcee man, his face showing smallpox scars. The Sarcee, a tribe of Déné Indians, migrated south from the boreal forest to the plains in the seventeenth and eighteenth centuries. Decimated recurrently by outbreaks of smallpox like all the other tribes of North America, the Sarcee finally established a home in the wooded foothills on a reserve near Calgary.
Photo by Ernest Brown, courtesy the Provincial Archives of Alberta.

A woman of the northern forest, circa 1900. Probably a member of one of the numerous Déné tribes that live in the boreal forests on both slopes of the Rockies, the Sekani to the west, the Beaver and the Chipewyan Indians on the Arctic drainage. Northern Indians adopted quickly the log structures Europeans introduced to North America. Note the careful dovetail notching of the corners.
Photo by C. W. Mathers, Ernest Brown Collection, courtesy the Provincial Archives of Alberta.

Kootenay camp on Canterbury Point, Lake Windermere, B.C., 1922. The fur trader David Thompson established Kootenae House near this point close to the headwaters of the Columbia River in 1807.
Photographer unknown, John Gibbon Collection, photo courtesy the Whyte Museum of the Canadian Rockies.

George McLean, Chief Walking Buffalo, Stoney, at Morley.
Photo by Harry Pollard, circa 1920, courtesy the Provincial Archives of Alberta.

John Hunter, Stoney, at the entrance to a Sundance lodge, his pipes, drums, and paraphernalia placed before him. The Sundance, an annual festival, lasts three or four days. Occurring near the summer solstice, the Sundance celebrates a belief in regenerate nature.
Photo by Byron Harmon, circa 1915, courtesy the Whyte Museum of the Canadian Rockies.

Mrs Enos Hunter, Stoney, with child on horse travois, circa 1930.
Photo by Byron Harmon, courtesy the Whyte Museum of the Canadian Rockies.

Stoney camp near Banff, Banff Indian Days, circa 1940.
Photo by Nicholas Morant, courtesy the photographer.

The Sundance lodge is built around a forked tree, the site of which is revealed to a seer, medicine man, or other individual. After the festival the site is abandoned.
Photo by Bruno Engler, circa 1950, courtesy the photographer.

Margaret Tenasse, Kootenay, and examples of her beadwork at her home near Windermere, B.C., circa 1945.
Photo by Nicholas Morant, courtesy the photographer.

Spectators at the Banff Indian Days rodeo found themselves intimately close to the action: bareback and saddle bronc busting, wild horse races, wild cow milking, Brahma bull riding, and calf-roping.
Photo by Bruno Engler, circa 1960, courtesy the photographer.

After the public events were over Indians pursued their own entertainment, playing the handgame. One player shifts an object from hand to hand, trying to mislead a guesser from the other team. In the picture Hanson Bearspaw is guessing while drummers accompany the game. Lying on the ground is the money being bet. The sticks before him indicate the current score. An expert player, Hanson Bearspaw greatly delighted in beating George Christou and Wally Dowhaniuk of the Banff Indian Days Association.
Photo by James Daubney, 1975, courtesy the photographer.

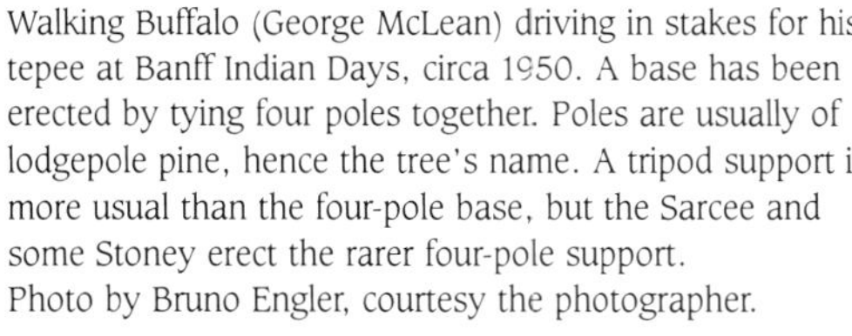

Walking Buffalo (George McLean) driving in stakes for his tepee at Banff Indian Days, circa 1950. A base has been erected by tying four poles together. Poles are usually of lodgepole pine, hence the tree's name. A tripod support is more usual than the four-pole base, but the Sarcee and some Stoney erect the rarer four-pole support.
Photo by Bruno Engler, courtesy the photographer.

The McLeans have almost finished erecting their tepee. Usually standing third among the tepees at the Banff Indian Days camp, it was among the most frequently photographed of all the tepees.
Photo by Bruno Engler, courtesy the photographer.

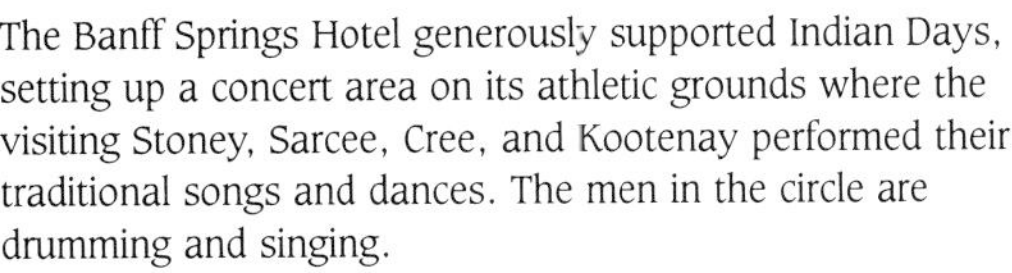

The Banff Springs Hotel generously supported Indian Days, setting up a concert area on its athletic grounds where the visiting Stoney, Sarcee, Cree, and Kootenay performed their traditional songs and dances. The men in the circle are drumming and singing.
Photo courtesy Canadian Pacific Archives.

Elizabeth Bearspaw, Stoney, circa 1945.
Portrait by Nicholas Morant, courtesy the photographer.

Mah-Min or The Feather, by Paul Kane. In 1840 the Stoney chief brought his people from their winter camp to Rocky Mountain House, where they met Robert Rundle and became Christians. Kane described the Stoney he met at Rocky Mountain House in 1848 as "the most kind and honourable of any tribe that I met with."
Oil on canvas, 76.2 x 63.2 cm.; courtesy the Montreal Museum of Fine Arts.

Catching Wild Horses, by Paul Kane. The people Kane depicts are likely Kootenay Indians who as late as the time of Kane's visit to the Columbia River country were still capturing horses to sell to the Plains Indians.
Oil on canvas, 45.7 x 73.7 cm.; courtesy the Royal Ontario Museum, Toronto.

Rocky Mountain House, by Paul Kane. Located in the lee of the Rockies, Rocky Mountain House, shown in the background of Kane's painting of a Stoney camp, was only a winter trading post by the 1840s. In his *Wanderings of an Artist* Kane says the Stoney tepees in his painting were ''formed entirely of pine branches.'' Here, before Kane visited the fort, the Stoney met the missionary Robert Rundle.
Oil on canvas, 45.7 x 73.7 cm.; courtesy the Royal Ontario Museum, Toronto.

Indians Playing at Alcoloh, by Paul Kane, circa 1848. The painter sketched Chualpays Indians at the game of Hoop and Dart west of the Rockies at Fort Colville on the Columbia River, the same game Peter Fidler described in his meeting with the Kootenay on the east side of the Rockies in 1789.
Oil on canvas, 45.7 x 73.7 cm.; courtesy the National Gallery of Canada.

Assiniboines Hunting Buffalo, by Paul Kane. The painter participated in a bison hunt near Fort Garry in 1845. In his traditional composition Kane combines his perceptions of the hunt and Assiniboine costumes.
Oil on canvas, 47 x 75.6 cm.; courtesy the National Gallery of Canada.

Hunting Bison on the Western Prairies, by Captain Henry James Warre, 1845. Watercolour wash.
Courtesy the Public Archives of Canada.

"At the base of Mount Rundle," 1845; a watercolour painting by Captain Henry James Warre.
Guided by Stoney Indians, the reconnaissance party of Warre and Lieutenant Mervin Vavasour
crossed the Rockies near Canmore, Alberta.
Courtesy the Public Archives of Canada.

McDougall Church, Morley, by Walter J. Phillips. John McDougall's church stands where the Methodist minister established his mission at Morleyville. The Stoney love the story of the man who tied his horse to a post during a blizzard. While he attended church, a chinook melted away the snow. After the service he found his horse dangling in its traces from the steeple.
Watercolour; courtesy the Banff Centre for Continuing Education.

Indian Days Camp, by Walter J. Phillips. The Banff artist, a master of watercolour and woodblock prints, and his students from the Banff School of Fine Arts often spent afternoons at the Indian Days encampment in the 1940s.
Colour woodblock print, 24.9 x 38.9 cm.; courtesy the Glenbow Museum.

"Tepees at the Kootenay Plains," photographer unknown, from a hand-tinted lantern slide; courtesy the Whyte Museum of the Canadian Rockies.

Chief David Bearspaw's Funeral, by Peter Whyte, 1956. The aged chief of the Bearspaw Band died in late February, 1956. The Stoney used such sleighs until the mid-sixties. Oil on canvas, 91.2 x 101 cm.; courtesy the Whyte Museum of the Canadian Rockies.

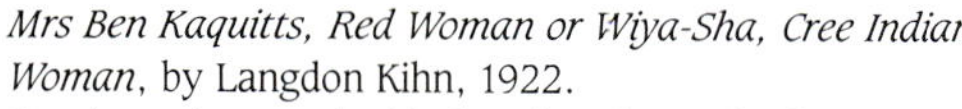

Mrs Ben Kaquitts, Red Woman or Wiya-Sha, Cree Indian Woman, by Langdon Kihn, 1922.
Her dress decorated with dentalia, the teeth of elk or deer, Mrs Kaquitts presents forceful stolidity in Langdon Kihn's portrait. She had married a Stoney. Kihn drew her portrait during Banff Indian Days.
Caran d'ache, approximately 60 x 45 cm.; private collection.

Susette, Kootenay Indian Woman, by Langdon Kihn, 1922.
The cradleboard in which the woman carries her baby shows both the traditional Kootenay love of horses and the floral motifs dominant in their beadwork.
Caran d'ache, approximately 60 x 45 cm.; courtesy the Glenbow Museum.

Indian Days Poster, 1923, by Langdon Kihn. The New York artist visited the Rockies under the sponsorship of the Canadian Pacific Railway in 1922, attending Indian Days in Banff and the David Thompson Centennial in Windermere, B.C. The Stoney and Kootenay portraits he drew during those festivals illustrated Marius Barbeau's *Indian Days in the Canadian Rockies*. Lithograph; courtesy the Whyte Museum of the Canadian Rockies.

Mrs Tom Simeon, by Peter Whyte, 1931.
The Stoney woman was about thirty years old when Peter Whyte painted her. He called the painting *The Red Squaw*; his widow retitled it in 1976.
Oil on canvas, 75 x 62.3 cm.; courtesy the Whyte Museum of the Canadian Rockies.

William Twin, by Peter Whyte, 1932. In his late eighties when he sat for the Whytes, the Stoney, William Twin, dressed in a capote, kept falling asleep. During the sittings he told the Whytes of his meeting Dr James Hector in the upper Bow Valley more than seventy years before.
Oil on canvas, 75 x 62.3 cm.; courtesy the Whyte Museum of the Canadian Rockies.

Mrs Jonie, by Peter Whyte, 1930. Mrs Jonie or Mrs Twoyoungman, a Stoney, was in her eighties at the time of the portrait.
Oil on canvas, 53.7 x 43.5 cm.; courtesy the Whyte Museum of the Canadian Rockies.

''Man with hawk,'' circa 1920;
handcoloured lantern slide, original photograph by Byron Harmon, courtesy the Whyte Museum of the Canadian Rockies.

''Man with drum,'' circa 1920,
handcoloured lantern slide, photographer unknown; courtesy the Whyte Museum of the Canadian Rockies.

Chief Dan Wildman, by Catharine Whyte, 1930. Peter and Catharine Whyte painted Dan Wildman and Mrs Jonie at Morley. When he came for his sitting Chief Wildman was dressed casually, but they prevailed upon him to dress in his ceremonial clothes. His necklace of grizzly teeth is made from the teeth of a bear he killed with a knife when he was about fifteen years old. Oil on canvas, 75 x 63 cm.; courtesy the Whyte Museum of the Canadian Rockies.

Hanson Bearspaw, handcoloured portrait by James Daubney.
Hanson Bearspaw, a Stoney, was a rancher, a wrangler, rodeo clown, a noted whip dancer, and an expert player of the handgame.
Photograph courtesy the artist.

Young Stoney Indians, photo by Byron Harmon, circa 1920,
hand-coloured by Carole Harmon, 1978. Courtesy the Whyte Museum of the Canadian Rockies.

Walking Buffalo, by Bruno Engler, circa 1960.
Born before the railroad reached the foothills, Walking Buffalo, George McLean, adopted by John Maclean, a missionary to the Bloods, was the first Stoney to obtain a secondary education. Both learned and witty, a medicine man among his people, the chief loved calling non-Indians "white savages."
Courtesy the photographer.

Horse race, Banff Indian Days, circa 1905.
The races and rodeo events were a major attraction for the participants in Banff Indian Days from its inception.
Photographer unknown, photo courtesy the Whyte Museum of the Canadian Rockies.

Stoney women watching the rodeo, Banff Indian Days, circa 1915.
The Stoney made their trips to Banff for the annual festival in such vehicles, taking two days for the journey.
Photo by Byron Harmon, courtesy the Whyte Museum of the Canadian Rockies.

Panoramic view of a Banff Indian Days parade, circa 1908.
Photographer unknown; photo courtesy the Whyte Museum of the Canadian Rockies.

Mrs Norman (Georgina) Luxton, Chief Hector Crawler, Norman Luxton, and Mrs Crawler, circa 1915.
The Crawlers' lives spanned the period from the mid-nineteenth century, through the signing of Treaty #7, the establishment of the Morley Reserve, the arrival of the railroad in the mountains in 1883, into the 1930s. Mrs Luxton, born at Morley, was the daughter of David McDougall, who established the first Morley store and was a brother of the missionary John McDougall. From 1915 to 1945 Norman Luxton was the driving force of Banff Indian Days.
Photo by Byron Harmon, courtesy the Whyte Museum of the Canadian Rockies.

Woman with children in Banff Indian Days parade, circa 1912.
Photo by Byron Harmon, courtesy the Whyte Museum of the Canadian Rockies.

Stoney tepees, Banff Indian Days, circa 1920.
In the nineteenth century the Stoney annually set up a camp at Minnehappa, the cascade for which the mountain behind the camp is named.
Photo by Byron Harmon, courtesy the Whyte Museum of the Canadian Rockies.

The Stoney were always glad to be part of Banff's festivals and events. For the Banff Winter Carnival, 1929, they erected their tepees on Banff Avenue.
Photo by Byron Harmon, courtesy the Whyte Museum of the Canadian Rockies.

Unknown photographer taking picture of Stoney children, Banff Indian Days, 1929.
Tom Wilson, in the Stetson, was an originator of the Banff festival.
Photographer unknown; photo courtesy the Whyte Museum of the Canadian Rockies.

Stoney women, Mary Dixon on the right, 1904. Photographer unknown; courtesy the Whyte Museum of the Canadian Rockies.

A moment later, their composure recovered for the photographer.

Susan Lefthand and child, circa 1930.
Portrait by Byron Harmon, courtesy the Whyte Museum of the Canadian Rockies.

Chief Buffalo Calf, Hector Crawler, Stoney, with Clifford White of Banff and his new Ludwig banjo.
An advertising card, circa 1925. Courtesy the Whyte Museum of the Canadian Rockies.

Young chicken dancers, in roaches of porcupine hair, await their turn to perform in the Indian Days evening concert.
Photo by Bruno Engler, courtesy the photographer.

Mary McLean of the Bearspaw Band and Catharine Whyte of Banff at Morley, Easter Monday, 1970, when the Stoney made Mrs Whyte, a painter and amateur historian, their sister, Princess White Shield. The bison on the medallion symbolizes the family of George McLean, Chief Walking Buffalo, Mary McLean's father. The two women met during Banff Indian Days in August, 1930. Catharine, a New Englander by birth who married the Banff artist Peter Whyte, called Mary her oldest Canadian friend.
Photo courtesy the *Calgary Herald*.

Jim Brewster and Norman Luxton of Banff caddying for Stoney chiefs, a gag shot set up for a postcard, circa 1935.
Photo by Byron Harmon, courtesy the Whyte Museum of the Canadian Rockies.

A scene from *Little Big Man*, Arthur Penn's adaptation of Thomas Berger's novel about the Battle of the Little Big Horn, filmed at Morley in 1969, the Stoney playing the roles of the Hunkpapa Sioux, and Canada's best-known Indian actor, Dan George, playing Old Lodgeskins.
Photo by Bruno Engler, courtesy the photographer.

Chief Jacob Twoyoungman poses for Ginger Rogers, 1939. Unseen by the camera, Mrs Morant holds Jacob's eagle feather headdress out for the photograph.
Photo by Nicholas Morant, courtesy the photographer.

Joshua and William Twin with Tom Wilson. William Twin, more than any other Stoney, involved himself in the development of tourism in the Rockies. Tom Wilson came to the Rockies with the railway surveys of 1882-83, and in 1889 he invited the Stoney to come to Banff to entertain Banff Springs Hotel guests, thus starting Banff Indian Days. Note the tepee made of recycled cement bags. Circa 1930.
Photographer unknown; photograph courtesy Canadian Pacific Corporate Archives, Montreal.

Epilogue

O, my sisters,
my sisters of the glowing dawn:
can you hear me, hear my song?
Or are you here? Or are you there?
Or are you gone forever,
travelling the sky to the east?

Here, or there, alas, or gone forever?

I see now the sun at the gateway of sunrise,
hear a voice,
the voice of the wind in the crags;
mighty the voice of the wind in its singing,
swaying the grass, the bushes, the fireweed, the tall trees:

"Listen, my son, do you hear my song?
I open my eyes, yet I cannot see you,
Twin sisters of sunrise,
I cannot see your glittering trail in the wind,
or the dust of your trail from afar.
When shall I hear you
singing again the song of all nature,
the wind carrying you,
picking flowers, grass, the trees' leaves as you drift?
When shall it be?

Dawn is near.
The wind is strong.
I wait, wait for a glimpse,
wait for a word,
one word that will save me."

adapted from a Salish Medicine Man's invocation, recorded by Marius Barbeau

Acknowledgments

Indians in the Rockies began with a request by the Banff Indian Days Association that I write a book to commemorate Banff Indian Days, a festival that held pride of place on Banff's calendar of events for almost ninety years. I argued, and the Association agreed readily, a book that placed Banff Indian Days in the context of the geography of Indian people in the Rockies would be more important, and more useful.

It's appropriate here to recognize all the people who have contributed to the success of Banff Indian Days. The Banff Indian Days Association gratefully thanks the chiefs and members of the Stoney, Sarcee, Cree, Blackfoot, Peigan, and Blood Tribes, without whose involvement, commitment, and participation the festival could not have been.

The Association wishes to acknowledge also the many Banff citizens who volunteered long hours before, during, and after the public events; the merchants and businesses in Banff, Lake Louise, and Canmore who donated goods, services, and funds; the service clubs of Banff—the Kiwanis, Lions, Rotary, and Kinsmen—which helped so much in background tasks; Parks Canada, whose co-operation kept things running smoothly; the officers and band of the Canadian Army Cadet Corps; Shaman Kitpou, who contributed enthusiastically to the festival, and who gave Banff the totem pole he carved during the 1976 festival; and all the sellers of Banff Indian Days coins, whose support of sales assured the festival's funding.

In more remote days—but also to be acknowledged—are Tom Wilson and my grandfather, Dave White, who aided the CPR in getting the event underway. Norman Luxton was the festival's mainstay for most of the years from 1915 to 1945. Peter and Catharine Whyte and my father, Dave White, did much of the running around to assure the festival's success in the middle and late 1940s. Claude Brewster was in charge for nearly two decades, until 1968, ably assisted by Miss Tilly Knight and Joe Squires, who gave freely of their time.

For the last years—1969 to 1978—a new generation of Banffites took over. Wally Dowhaniuk was chairman for those years, and Jim Parker and Jim Santa Lucia acted as vice-chairmen. Gordon DeBoice and Joe Balog sought donations of food and handled the distribution of rations. Bus Rivett, who'd involved himself in the running of events from the early 1950s, continued to be master of ceremonies for rodeo and cultural events. At the final afternoon show of Banff Indian Days in 1978 the gathered tribes recognized the contributions of Wally and Bus by bestowing honorary chiefhoods upon them. Wally, who had spent so many dawn hours at the campsite arousing the people for the parades, became Chief Morning Whistler. Bus, whose sonorous voice drew the day's events to a close, became Chief Twilight Bugler.

The Association gratefully acknowledges other members of the committee and their contributions. George Mandryk devoted long days to gate control at the Indian Days Grounds, accounting for every cent of income, then turning it over to George Christou, who paid the money out to the Indians for their participation in events. George Christou also managed the Indian Days coin sales, a vital source of revenue as expenses for the festival rose in the 1970s. Don Henderson was responsible for grounds maintenance and cleanup; Craig Rothwell and Frank Vegesi served as treasurers; Bob Davies and Don Hawthorne were parade marshals; and Pat Parker and her family registered each participating individual entering the grounds. John Pawluk kept community relations running smoothly, sometimes during rocky days.

Without the help of all those people Banff Indian Days could not have succeeded.

My thanks to Marlene Alt, who undertook willingly a vast amount of research reading for me; Joyce Johnson, who read the manuscript critically and well at an early stage; Brian Patton, who suggested a number of lines of inquiry and who graciously loaned me the transcription of Peter Fidler's journal he had painstakingly copied in the Public Archives of Canada; my cousin Clifford A. White, who drew attention to his own research on forest fire and burning patterns in the Bow Valley and the work of Stephen Barrett in Montana; Don Gardner, who brought his archaeological and geological awarenesses to bear on the chapter on Paleo-Indians; Al McClelland, who discussed bead art at length with me; Craig Richards of the Whyte Museum of the Canadian Rockies, who strived for excellence in the reproduction prints for the black-and-white portfolios of the book; Edward Cavell of the same institution, who prepared most of the reproductions of its paintings; Patricia Ainsley of the Glenbow Museum, who drew my attention to that institution's collection of Langdon Kihn portraits; Mrs Hal Bavin of Invermere, British Columbia, who loaned me her husband's negatives of Kootenay portraits; Bruno Engler, whose enthusiasm for the project led him into negative envelopes he hadn't looked into for two decades; Anthony Perzel of Canmore; and Mr and Mrs Nicholas Morant, whose assistance is always freely given and whose personal friendship I consider one of the prizes given for living in Banff.

I must particularly thank Wally Dowhaniuk and the Banff Indian Days Association for their enthusiasm for this book and their co-operation in seeing it through to publication, and Carole Harmon and Stephen Hutchings at Altitude Publishing, who are not satisfied with less than excellence, and Martin and Jane Lynch, who trimmed my excesses but allowed me my flourishes.

Jon Whyte

The Banff Indian Days Association: Bus Rivett, George Christou, Wally Dowhaniuk, George Mandryk and Jim Santa Lucia, circa 1980, courtesy the Banff Indian Days Association

Joe Smallboy, Jr., 1975. In July, 1965, Robert Smallboy led his band of Cree from Hobbema, Alberta, to a wilderness location near the Cline River in the Rockies, a return to their traditional lifestyle from the constraints of the reservation. His son, Joe, and the Smallboy band participated in Banff Indian Days in the early 1970's.
Photographer unknown; courtesy of the Banff Indian Days Association.

Banff Indian Days Souvenir Coins. The Kiwanis Club and the Indian Days Association had coins minted annually, both to promote the festival and to raise funds for the events. Charlie Beil, a well-known Banff sculptor, designed the coins through 1976.

Totem pole by Shaman Kitpou. The Ontario chief carved the pole during Banff Indian Days, and the Association erected it in downtown Banff.
Photograph by Jim Santa Lucia.

Bibliography

All unpublished materials included in the Bibliography are in the collections of the Whyte Museum of the Canadian Rockies: Archives; Banff, Alberta.

Allen, Samuel E.S., "Mountaineering in the Canadian Rockies," *The Alpine Journal,* Vol. XVIII, 1897; pp. 96-120, 222-236, 397-402

Banff *Crag and Canyon.* The accounts concerning the Stoney and Banff Indian Days appear in issues in the third or fourth week of July when Banff Indian Days occurred. The account of Hector Crawler's encounter with the train appeared January 29, 1916.

Barbeau, Marius, *Indian Days in the Canadian Rockies,* Toronto, 1923.

Barbeau, Marius, *Indian Days on the Western Prairie,* Ottawa, 1960.

Barrett, Stephen W., "Ethnohistory of Indian Fire Practices in Western Montana," School of Forestry, University of Montana.

Barrett, Stephen W., "Indian Fire" in *Western Wildlands*, Spring 1980, Vol VI, No. 3, pp 17-21.

Brody, Hugh, *Maps and Dreams*, Vancouver, 1981.

Christensen, O.A., *1969 Archaeological Survey of Banff National Park.*

Culin, Stewart, *Games of the North American Indians*, originally the accompanying paper to the *Twenty-Fourth Annual Report of the Bureau of American Ethnology to the Smithsonian Institution, 1902-1903* in 1907, Washington, reprinted New York, 1975.

Elliott, Jack, *Jasper National Park and Ya-Ha-Tinda Ranch, Archaeological Survey, Preliminary Report, 1970.*

Fedje, Daryl, "Banff Archaeological Project 1983 – An Overview."

Gryba, Eugene M., *Sibbald Creek: 11,000 years of human use of the Alberta Foothills, Archaeological Survey of Alberta, 1983.*

Harkin, J.B., letter to James Simpson, July 23, 1921.

Interior Report, 1886, "Mr. Whitcher's Report," December 31, 1886, Ottawa, Department of the Interior.

Kane, Paul, *Paul Kane's Frontier,* edited by J. Russell Harper, Toronto, 1971.

Loy, Thomas H., "Report of an Archaeological Survey, Yoho National Park," 1972.

Maclean, John, *McDougall of Alberta,* Toronto, 1927

Mackenzie, Alexander, *Journals and Letters of Alexander Mackenzie,* edited by W. Kaye Lamb, Toronto, 1970.

McDougall, John, *On Western Trails in the Early Seventies,* Toronto, 1911.

Morris, Alexander, *The Treaties of Canada with the Indians of Manitoba, the North-West Territories, and Kee-wa-tin in the Dominion of Canada,* Toronto, 1880.

Roe, Frank Gilbert, *The Indian and the Horse,* Norman, Oklahoma, 1955.

Schaeffer, Claude E., "Plains Kutenai; An Ethnological Evaluation," *Alberta History,* Autumn, 1982, pp. 1-9.

Schäffer, Mary T.S., *Old Indian Trails,* New York, 1911.

Simpson, Sir George, *Narrative of a Journey Round the World,* London, 1847.

Spry, Irene, *The Palliser Papers 1857-60,* Champlain Society, Toronto, 1968.

Thompson, David, *David Thompson's Narrative,* edited by Richard Glover, Toronto, Champlain Society, 1962.

Warren, Mary T.S. [Schäffer], "Lake Louise of Early Days," unpublished account.

Whyte, Catharine Robb, unpublished letters and notes, 1930-1979.

Wilcox, Walter D., *Camping in the Canadian Rockies,* New York, 1896.

Wilcox, Walter D., *The Rockies of Canada,* New York, 1909.

About the Author

Jon Whyte, portrait by Craig Richards.

Born and raised in Banff, Jon Whyte is a member of a family that has been associated for almost 100 years with the mountain resort town and the Stoney Indians of the area. In writing *Indians in the Rockies,* he has drawn from his own vivid memories, the recollections of his family, and the remarkable cultural heritage that forms the Whyte Museum of the Canadian Rockies.

An innovative, award-winning poet, Jon Whyte has written and collaborated on many other books of Rocky Mountain interest, including *Rocky Mountain Madness* with Edward Cavell, and *Lake Louise: A Diamond in the Wilderness* with Carole Harmon, both of which were produced by Altitude Publishing. He is a columnist for the Banff weekly newspaper, *The Crag and Canyon*, and is the Curator of the Heritage Collection of the Whyte Museum of the Canadian Rockies in Banff.

Once upon a time, more than a hundred centuries ago, campfires burned in the Rocky Mountains near the site of the mountain village of Banff. Today, tourists driving the Trans-Canada Highway west from Calgary little suspect that they follow one of the oldest trails in North America.

Indians in the Rockies traces the silent tread of mankind in the mountains, from the Paleo-Indians at the dawn of human habitation in southern Canada to the modern mountain tribes who learned to subsist and survive in the valleys of the Rockies. We view history from the perspective of European culture; it is astonishing to realize the extent to which we are newcomers to the mountains. As white civilization crept westward it was the mountain Indians who revealed the secrets of the high passes and guided the explorers and fur traders in their search for an east-west route through the mountain barrier.

The story of the mountain Indians is a crazy quilt pieced together from legends and mountain lore, explorers' journals, archaeological reports and missionaries' memoirs. A modern focus is provided by a detailed description of the Stoney Indians, who have been mountain dwellers for the last two centuries. From 1889 to 1978 they shared their ceremonies, celebrations and games through a unique annual festival, Banff Indian Days.

Indians in the Rockies is richly illustrated with photographs, drawings and paintings which provide a visual counterpoint to the text. Together text and images weave a rich portrait of a fascinating chapter in the history of Canada's native peoples.